LIVING ISLAM

LIVING ISLAM
EAST & WEST

Shaykh Fadhlalla Haeri

ELEMENT BOOKS

in association with

ZAHRA PUBLICATIONS

First published in 1989 by
Element Books Limited
Longmead, Shaftesbury, Dorset

Printed and bound in Great Britain
by Billings, Hylton Road, Worcester

Cover design by Max Fairbrother

Cover illustration: Jeremy Norton

British Library Cataloguing in Publication Data

Haeri, Fadhlalla
Living Islam
1. Islamic life
I. Title
297'.44

I S B N 1 - 85230 - 065 - 5

Contents

Acknowledgements

This book evolved out of a series of diverse talks given, as the title suggests, in the East and the West. Gratitude and thanks are due to Hajj Abbas Taylor, Hajj Ahmad Mikell and Dr. Abdul Wahab Boase for editing all the material into its present form.

Ahmed

1

The Recovery of Spiritual Values

Everybody is at a loss except those who understand the nature of man's capacity to fall into loss and thus act correctly. Correct action means for the sake of Allah, anything else is not correct action. Our mission is only to know the reality of Allah. If we aim for that, we will achieve everything else. If we merely try and explain aspects of Islam, we will always be at a loss. If we aim for Allah, we will understand everything, but if we only go for bits and pieces, we will always have divided opinions. In every so-called Muslim country there are factions and people at odds with one another because they are Muslims by name, but not Muslims by heart and action, and this is the situation everywhere in the world, not only in Muslim countries but in Christian countries, in Hindu countries, in Buddhist countries, and in countries where there is no religion. The reason for this is simple: they are not living this life for Allah and for the next life they do not remember death.

Allah in Arabic is the Majestic Name. It has no attribute, rather it indicates the essence. Attributes are all of the qualities we can witness: the Powerful, the Giver, the Taker, the One before us, the One after us, the One who gives life. All of these are attributes of Allah. Creation is Allah's action. In order to find out the meaning of good and bad, we must start with creation. We begin from the physical, and find that it is relative and not acceptable, because it is ever-changing. For example, the child begins to experiment with his immediate environment because he wants to connect with everything around him, he wants to assimilate all that he encounters. This search at the existential level takes the form of searching for cause and effect relationships.

Islam, meaning 'submission', is complete understanding and unification with the reality of existence. We are actually already unified with that reality, but we do not know it because we see separation and boundaries. As a global community, we have different habits, different languages and different cultures, but in truth, we are all created from one self. The Qur'an says,

We have created you from one self.

(4:1)

Self *(nafs)* means all of the different character manifestations and feelings each one of us have. Self means the attributes, feelings and experience which all of us share. We all know the meaning of peace and love and hate and insecurity. We all know the meaning of fear and pain and hunger. We all experience heat and cold. In fact, everything we experience is based on opposites. You cannot have life without death. God cannot be experienced without the knowledge of evil, nor friendship without enemies. Adulthood cannot be experienced without the experience of childhood. There is day and night, high and low, man and woman. All of these we experience in our lives. This is the meaning of one self.

Also, we have a faculty in us, the faculty of reason. That faculty must be nourished as we grow. We are all programmed to want to know more, and if we do not continue to know more, we suffer. We all want to be in harmony in this life, which is a preparation for the next life. Ultimately, we will come to know that there is only One Reality behind all this. This is the meaning of "There is no god but Allah". The statement is easy, very easy. All religions, all men seeking enlightenment say "There is no god but Allah". Anybody who contemplates, meditates or sits quietly, after a while sees one hand behind everything. What is difficult is "Muhammad is the Messenger of Allah". The wisdom of seeing One we can obtain quickly. The problem is what to do next. This is where differences occur. How are we going to devise the best type of society in this world? All of the Prophets have tried, in their respective times, to teach the people of their society the most suitable way to live. Each Prophet embodied the teachings of those before him and brought a system that was particularly applicable to the needs of his time. Some prophets did not prohibit the use of wine because it was one of the most important foods that the people had. As they pressed the grapes for juice it became wine in the hot weather. Certain factors made it necessary to prohibit the intake of alcohol during the Prophet Muhammad's time, one of which certainly must have been that alcoholic intoxication had become a serious problem among the Arabs and was due to remain a social problem in the future as we witness in our own time. We raise this matter here because it is an example of a prophetic law, and therefore a Divine Law, which differed from what came before. It is a law which many people could not and cannot follow, thus cutting them off from the Path to Reality. The Prophet said: "I am the city of knowledge," so access to knowledge is obtained emulating and imitating his way. He further said: "And 'Ali is its gate (the gate to the city of knowledge). Whoever enters a city must enter by it's gate."

The Prophet Muhammad spent a lot of time with 'Ali, and 'Ali asked him many many questions which clarified the prophetic knowledge. The knowledge of 'Ali and his descendants (the Imams and the *Ahl al-Bayt*) is the same knowledge as that of Muhammad. It only serves to explain the teachings of Muhammad. To give you an example, at the time of the Prophet people had few clothes, thus holes were mended with patches and the clothes continued to be worn until they were threadbare. Everybody lived like this. After the Prophet, people seeking to imitate him continued to wear patched clothing even though Arabia had become extremely wealthy. During the time of Imam Ja'far as-Sadiq, a person came to him and asked, "Why do you dress so well when your great-grandfather wore patched clothes." He said, "At that time there was nothing else. Now everybody has these clothes. I dress like everybody else. I don't want to be different. The Prophet said that one should dress as the people do." And then the Imam said, "If it was for me I would wear what I have underneath." And he showed a cloth underneath which was all patched.

These teachings have come down to us from the Prophet, but since he did not have time to elaborate and explain them, this task was left to the *Ahl al-Bayt*. This is the difference between Shi'ah and Sunni Islam. In reality there is no difference, it is only a matter of dogma. We want to reach Allah and we know that the quickest way to Allah is the way of Muhammad. In order to understand Muhammad, we need to understand his family, for the Prophet enjoined this upon us. This then is the school of the *Ahl al-Bayt*. It makes the teachings of Muhammad easier and more accessible. If we are not interested in knowing the laws of God, we will always have disagreements and disputes.

Those who seek the knowledge of God gather together so that they can determine how best to live life successfully, nobly, honourably, and in harmony. They meet in order to prepare for the next experience which is death.

Let us examine the situation in Japan, for instance, to see how a spiritual tradition, which was until recently deeply rooted among the people, is beginning to decline. Many of the good habits of the people have become mere rituals which have lost their meaning. Family life is not as strong now as it was twenty years ago. The same is true of loyalty to one's friend and one's employer and morality in general. There is much decadence and corruption. Before, in this country, sport was for people to participate in. Now it has become spectator-oriented because it is copying the decadent West. Tradition now has become a once-a-year annual event. Husbands and wives may dress up in traditional dress only once in their lifetime for a photograph. Values and practices are imported from the West and the old values are no longer nurtured. Traditional Japanese values are those of Islam: honesty, openness, loyalty, love for family, humility, modesty. Women traditionally placed their husbands before themselves, and were subservient and obedient. The situation in the West is not like this and this erosion of values has affected countries throughout the world. The Arab countries where Islam began and grew have lost their traditions and have become arrogant. They have become fat. All the rulers of the Arab countries are dictators. This has nothing to do with Islam. The only Islam is an attempt in Iran which was the most decadent and corrupt country in the Middle East until the Islamic Revolution. Now they are hoping to change, but this change takes time. Fifty years of corruption is not wiped away in five years. We hope and pray for its success, because if the attempt succeeds, then many other countries can learn from it.

Japanese culture was based on modesty and contentment. The influx of decadent western values began in 1953 with Commodore Perry. It is alright to have Commodore perry if the culture is strong in its inner meaning. The Shoguns knew that the code of conduct was not strong enough and that is why they wanted to close the country. Japan is now bowing to the West and does not really wish to do so, so there is conflict. The Japanese personality is facing a crisis.

It is not true that the Shoguns vanished in 1867. The Shogun is still there. He is in the White House. He pays his respects to the Emperor. However, only one Emperor can rule. A nation will not be one nation under one rule unless it rules itself. Islam rules the self. The Muslim believes that man has the capacity to be God's representative on this earth, if he is just, compassionate, wise, and his body and his soul are in harmony, if he is ready to serve and wants to bring peace for everybody. The Muslim believes that eventually everyone will realize that the way to live in this world is peacefully with few desires and much service, positive service, not just running around aimlessly, chasing a little golf ball. The prosperity of towns in Japan can now be measured by whether or not they have a golf course.

In traditional Japanese culture when men became old, they were considered the most important member of the family. The children loved to be with them, and they taught because they had reached a high degree of wisdom. They had stopped chasing after business and material success because they had become older and wiser. In modern Japan, when a person becomes old, he is sent out on a golf course to chase after a ball. It is therapy for the decadent West. Man's life is supposed to be balanced. He should not expose himself to an office environment for so long that he has to go out and get drunk to forget about the madness he is in. This situation is that of the world in general, not just of Japan.

Islam is the therapy for all mankind. The Qur'an says the Prophet, may the peace and blessings of Allah be upon him and his family, was 'A Mercy for all the worlds' (21:107). Every teaching that came before Islam is within Islam. We say that every child is born a Muslim until his parents change him, because the child is natural and in a state of submission.

If the Muslims who truly understand the meaning of Islam can show the Qur'an and the way of Muhammad to people all over the world in a digestible form, then they will have provided a great service. Allah will love them because they will be doing His work, which is to save man from his own ignorance.

2
Remembrance of Allah

The basic principle of *dhikr* (remembrance or invocation of Allah) is to bring oneself into a state in which there are no thoughts, thereby becoming neutralized and cleansed. At first it is difficult. We are distracted by many thoughts and memories. Eventually, we should reach a point in which we are clear and without thoughts.

There are many techniques which may be used to achieve this state. One which I find very useful is thinking of the word 'Allah' in Arabic. As an aid you can picture yourself writing it. But remember, it is just a technique to exclude thoughts. Another method is to visualize yourself within the black stone, with absolutely no colour and nothing that you can discern. The objective is to become neutralized. The Qur'an says:

> So when you are free (emptied), still toil.
>
> (94:7)

Faragha in this *ayah* means 'empty', empty of what matters, which are thoughts. It is very difficult to do.

I will give you an example of how difficult it is to achieve, even for a great man of knowledge. Imam Ghazzali asked his mother why his brother Ahmad had never prayed behind him. Imam Ghazzali was a teacher and scholar, and had a large number of followers and belonged to a Sufi order or *tariqah* (literally path). Imam Ghazzali wondered why people came from all over the world to pray behind him yet his brother had never done so. Later, their mother asked Shaykh Ahmad to please pray behind his brother. So one day he and his few disciples *(murids)* came to the great mosque in Baghdad where thousands of people had gathered. In the second *rak'ah* (a part of the prayer) behind Imam Ghazzali, Shaykh Ahmad suddenly left the prayer. A few of his followers, bewildered, did the same. This created a great disturbance in the mosque. When Shaykh Ahmad was approached and asked, "Why did you leave the prayer, what happened?" he replied: "In the second *rak'ah* you did not have an Imam, he had left you." The people, very disturbed, asked Imam

Ghazzali if what Shaykh Ahmad had said was true, that he had
left them in the prayer. He replied: "Regretfully, he speaks the
truth; my mind did wander off in the second *rak'ah* ."

As another example of the difficulty of controlling the thoughts
that enter the mind, I mention the following story told by a great
Shaykh from Turkey named Shaykh Muzaffar:

Not long ago in Istanbul a *majdhub* (a man mad in Allah)
happened to be praying behind a famous scholar. Suddenly, in
the middle of the prayer, the . *majdhub*) started screaming, "My
stick is under the apple tree, my stick is under the apple tree!"
This was quite disturbing to everyone. Later, some of the men
went after him determined to harm him. The Imam said, "No,
please do not do anything to him. Leave him alone because the
disturbance during the prayer came from my mind. It suddenly
occurred to me whilst I was praying that yesterday I had left
my stick under an apple tree in an orchard."

The only way that the thoughts in one's mind can be controlled
is through awareness. There is a famous story about a rascal
who lived in India during the reign of a king who had lost all
his hair. As a consequence his queen no longer cared for him
and he desperately sought help to grow his hair back. The rascal
came to the king and assured him that he could cure him. The
king replied, "I am willing to spend whatever it takes to find a
cure. The only thing that is important to me in this life is that
my hair should grow back." The men told the king that he could
help him, but there would be many conditions. The king eagerly
agreed to everything he wanted.

First, the clever man mobilized the king's entire army to gather
herbs from specific places in a complicated fashion that looked
very impressive. He arranged to be given a whole wing of the
palace in which to live and prepare his elixirs. The king went
to a great deal of expense, and finally, after a long wait, was
told that his remedy was ready.

"You must rub this medicine on your head three times a day
for forty days," instructed the rascal to the king. "But there is
one simple condition: when you rub it in, you must not think of
three things — spinach, buttons, and roast chicken." "That will
be easy," said the king, "I hate spinach, I don't even have buttons

on my clothes and roast chicken is not among my favourites."
"If you do think of any of those things," the trickster said, "you
must begin the treatment again for the full forty consecutive
days. It is fully guaranteed."

For three years the king tried in vain to carry out his promise
but each time, after twenty or so days had passed, he would
inevitably say to himself, "Oh, what was it that I was not supposed to think of?" The rascal had successfully swindled the king.

The point of this story is that it is impossible to refrain from
thinking, and therefore, it is necessary to find an image, like
Allah's name, the black stone or any other thing that helps us
to obliterate our thoughts. It is impossible not to think. Our
objective is to be in a pure state of consciousness, which is not
easy, but which can be achieved through practice.

The reason for the circles in the recitation of *dhikr* (invocation,
rememberance) is to help us to practise being in a state of full
alertness and wakefulness, yet without thoughts. It is very re-
freshing and rejuvenating. It is energizing and it gives us a new
state of elation. That is the purpose of *dhikr*. It is not a superstitious exercise, rather it has a direct effect, that of purifying our
hearts, making them turn. The *dhikr* causes us to turn from a state
of thought to one of non-thought and back again. By this we are
neutralized, refreshed, and ready to accept anything again in life.

Remembrance is a technique for overcoming the self which is
constantly under strain. As a matter of course, the self manifests
a certain measure of doubt. Allah's statement:

> Now surely by Allah's remembrance are the hearts
> set at rest.
>
> (13:28)

addresses this propensity of the self. Thinking of Allah means
not thinking of other than Allah. In a way, everything else we
can think of can be considered other than Allah. This is not
Allah, and yet it is created by the decree of Allah.

Through subtlety we find that we only see Allah. Even when
hit upon the head we are wont to say, 'Praise be to Allah! Yes,
I realize I should not be here. I was in the wrong place at the
wrong time.' To reach this state a neutralizing factor is needed.

When people do *dhikr* — if they are the right people, performing it for the right purpose, in the right way — this is the result.

Recite *dhikr* as loud as you like. The sound is important, it helps to overcome the thoughts. Try to be as comfortable as possible so that you can forget your body and yourself. The object of this is to be nowhere. Not sitting comfortably indicates that later your circulation of blood in certain areas of your body may be hindered. So be as relaxed as possible. Generally, because of the electric and magnetic currents in our body, it is very useful to keep your hands touching. We will find most Sufi paths place the right hand on top of the left; somehow that helps to neutralize the body.

The more we practise, the more we find that the best position is to sit cross-legged with the spine erect. You may prop yourself up or sit in a chair to achieve a relaxed position. Ultimately, most of the paths of Sufism take a person into what is called *khalwah* (seclusion, retreat) or *i'tikaf* (retreat at specific times). *Khalwah* and *i'tikaf* have a certain etiquette surrounding them. Generally speaking, *i'tikaf* refers to the last ten days of Ramadan when one may remain confined within the precincts of the mosque, but it also means to have taken refuge, to have isolated one's self in order to attain the state of purification. In any case, the more we practise, the more we can do it any time, anywhere.

There are various methods of helping to subdue our thoughts during *dhikr*. One way is not to attack them. We allow them to come out and be looked at. If a thought is disturbing to us, we do not suppress it, for that would only confirm it more. Allow the thoughts to come out, greet it, salute it and then dismiss it as if you were a sergeant major in charge of inspecting his soldiers. Recognize one bad aspect of each soldier and move on to the next, until the parade of thoughts passes you by completely and you are no longer distracted. Incidentally, we must be in *wudu';* not being in *wudu'* may cause us to become distracted.

When this occurs, the ultimate subtlety, which is in the form of energy, becomes manifest. When the subtle *(latif)* and dense *(kathif)*, the light and the sound, become so connected at the same time, the subtle becomes more subtle, almost obivious as one approaches the nondescript state of no-thought.

I hope these words will be helpful to you whenever you sit and do *dhikr*. The more we dive into it the more it will become second nature to us; and the *dhikr* may be resumed at whatever stage we left off.

Another suggestion which is useful for the early stages of the practise when you are very agitated, is to think of yourself sitting in front of a very calm sea, looking at the horizon. Then think of the name of Allah emerging slowly from it, getting bigger and bigger. This technique helps to focus one's thoughts. At the end of a session of *dhikr* it is useful to do the *dhikr* very quietly. Most of the Naqshabandi *tariqahs* (orders, paths) end their *dhikr* with almost twenty minutes of complete silence. The idea is to obtain the maximum benefit from it. After we have quieted our minds completely, we just stay still. We can paint the name in our hearts so that it remains the point of tranquillity from which we can benefit during the day.

I would like now to talk about things of interest to the businessman. There are a great deal of misconceptions and mis-understandings about the meaning of *dunya* (the material world) and what it is; as well as about wealth and poverty. I am going to read from a collection of hadiths which I have gathered and which, I hope very much, will one day be translated into Malay. It is a very brief collection covering matters that concern the person on the path. It is broken down into sections by topic. There is no commentary, only ayats from the Qur'an and hadiths. So it can serve as a foundation for knowledge. I shall give you some idea of it, so that you may see if it appeals to you. I would like to read from a section which defines many of the key terms within Islam, beginning with *shukr* (gratefulness). The Qur'an says:

> If you are grateful, I would certainly give to you more.
>
> (14:7)

How does this work? How does man obtain increase, as the Qur'an says, from gratitude? Well, we may say that if a businessman is grateful for his business he will make more business and thereby be more successful. How does this come about?

Let us look at it this way: the moments we are in *shukr* will be the moments in which we will find increase — any ordinary person, any unbeliever who is grateful will also find increase. Even the worst disbeliever, who does not pray, but who has the state of gratitude will benefit from it. Many of the unbelievers have absorbed aspects of our great heritage of Islam without even knowing it, but they greatly benefit from them. The moment a person is in *shukr* his heart is contained and content. Suppose a child wants a bicycle. The desire for the bicycle is an agitation which vanishes as soon as he receives the object. His state becomes one of complete contentment. The state of contentment is good for us because within it our energies are preserved and we are whole.

The believer's nature is to be content with knowledge. This should be our aim. Man's normal state is discontentment because he wants to go back to Allah and maintain the perfect eternal situation. If he experiences something good, he wants it to be preserved forever. If what he experiences is bad, he wants it to vanish. But, of course, this is not possible in this world. Allah says:

> What troubles my slaves is that they seek comfort
> in this life and I did not create it for comfort.

He created this world so that we are constantly sparked and thereby constantly evolving.

When we are satisfied we have no agitation, no desires, we are whole. At that moment we are most efficient, and therefore, we will have a greater possibility of succeeding. Psychologically, this is the most efficient state because our thoughts are contained, thereby allowing us to better project our will.

Therefore, the state of gratitude is a state of inner tranquillity and balance. All our faculties are present — our senses and our faculty of reasoning — and because of that we will correctly judge the situations that confront us, bringing success. The section on *shukr* is two pages long but, as I said, it is a very simple formula based solely on traditions without a commentary.

The book contains another section on the qualities of character. What is missing in these modern times is the knowledge of be-

haviour. There is a great deal of interest in Islam but not sufficient knowledge which is easily available to us on human conduct. In one section there are traditions concerning the meaning of 'the best character', humility, modesty, and forgiveness, as well as obliteration. In Arabic, when we say 'excuse me', 'forgive me', we are saying 'please obliterate the time in which wrong was committed'. There are four Arabic words for generosity, one of them is *sakha'*. Each one is covered as well as 'humility', 'honour', 'abstinence', 'fear', 'hope', 'wealth', and 'poverty'.
'hope', 'wealth', and 'poverty'.

There are several ayats and traditions on the meaning of wealth and poverty. Allah says in *Surah al-Duha:*

> Did He not find you in want and free you from want.
>
> (93:8)

He is specifically addressing the Prophet, but if we are lovers of the Prophet and his followers, it is also applicable to us. If an *ayah* of Qur'an were only a message to the Prophet, there would be no point in our reading it. But, in fact, every *ayah* of the Qur'an applies to us. When Allah says:

> Perdition will overtake both hands of Abu Lahab, and he will perish.
>
> (111:1)

it means not only that Abu Lahab, who seems to be powerful, will die, but that each one of us who acts in the manner of Abu Lahab will perish and be at a loss in the same way that Abu Lahab was. In this world there are many Abu Lahabs.

The Qur'an is not a historical document, it is a manual for existence. If we do not treat the Qur'an as such, we have missed the point. The Qur'an says:

> Allah has found you in want.
>
> (93:8)

Everyone of us has been in trouble, uncertain and insecure and

has then been enriched. By simply remembering this we will
witness nature's perfection. Allah's perfect way has fallen upon
each one of us, giving us greater confidence and certainty. Last
year each one of us had problems. Where are these problems
now? They have gone. And tomorrow we will have new problems.
The Qur'an says in another *ayah:*

> If they are needy, Allah will make them free from
> want out of His grace.
>
> (24:32)

If a person admits his failings and poverty, Allah will enrich
him with His bounty. As you know, enrichment may be of a
physical or a spiritual kind. Outwardly we may be well, but
inwardly bereft. A person may have a great deal of wealth, but
be very unhappy. In fact, this is usually the case, because we
cannot become very wealthy unless we have invested a great
deal of time and effort that could have been spent on the inner
life. There is a formula which states that we cannot have it all.
There are a limited number of days and just so much energy for
all of us.

If, when we are in poverty, we admit our poverty, there is the
possibility of coming out of it. Our recognition will cause us to
investigate our situation. We will ask, 'Is it our land? Is it our
resources?' We will have the freedom, within limitations, to do
something about it. Of course, we are not free to live forever,
but we are free to care for our health; in fact, it is our duty,
otherwise, we would be washed-out fatalistic people.

We are simultaneously enslaved and free, constricted, and yet
able to act within certain constrictions. If we recognize the
bounds of the *shari'ah* (the body of Islamic law), we act within
them. This life is Allah's melting pot which tests whether or not
we have the power of reasoning that can recognize the bounds
of right and wrong within the *shari'ah.*

If we recognize the source and the root of poverty, we will be
able to do something about it or, finding it impossible to do
anything, make the best of it. We will not experience agitation
and we will know that we have done our utmost, which is in

itself an enrichment. The abundance and mercy of Allah is, in this case, the recognition of one's total situation.

The grace of Allah manifests in a variety of ways. The Prophet said: "The dinar and the dirham have caused the destruction of many people before and you will cause your destruction." Imam 'Ali was asked, "What is the meaning of dirham (currency)?" He replied: "It is derived from *dar al-ham* (the house of grief)." They asked him, "What is dinar?" and he replied: "It is from *dar al-nar* (house of fire)." Fire has many uses. We can prepare food with it, but it can also engulf us. So watch out for the dirham and the dinar.

In another hadith from the Prophet related by Imam Baqir: "There are from amongst my believing slaves those whose religious or spiritual affairs will not be completed unless they are in wealth and in expansion, and in good health in their bodies; so I will afflict them with wealth and good health and expansion, so that their spiritual affairs become appropriate for them. And there are other believing slaves whose affairs will not be put right except by poverty."

In Arabic, the *misqin* is defined as he who does not know from where his next meal is coming, and who suffers from ill health. It is by this situation that his spiritual affairs improve. Allah says, "I know what is best for My believing slaves." Another tradition which is similar to the one which we have mentioned says, "Allah will bring some people to the Garden on bleeding knees and chains, while others He will bring in dignity." These traditions indicate that if a person has true faith, he will recognize his situation to be perfect for him.

If a man is truly a believer, he believes that his duty is to learn to know the way of Allah, and that he is always encompassed by Allah. If there is anything in it that he does not recognize as being in full balance, he should ask Allah for a way out, for Allah is the Most Merciful; and he should do his best to change his situation.

Then of course, he might not know what to do, or how to change his situation. For example, if a man wants to improve his material existence, he might go to a new place and plunge himself into establishing a business, because that is what he knows how to do. When he loses all his money, he will say, 'Allah is unkind to me.' But in truth, he was not sufficiently knowledgeable or discriminating. He did not first survey the market properly and therefore was unprepared. It is ignorance he should blame not Allah, for Allah is above blame. The believer is he who either knows that he is afflicted by his own ignorance and is content with it, or believes he will come to know what is necessary to remedy his situation. His belief is not blind, it is direct witnessing. The Qur'an says:

> Say: Are the blind and the seeing one alike?
> (6:50)

'Seeing' means knowledge, insight and correct knowledge; and the more we know, the more we find out how little we know.

Obtaining knowledge of the physical world is very easy to obtain. It is very basic. The physical world is but a small portion of existence composed of many other worlds which we do not perceive. There are millions of worlds whose wave bands are being transported through space, each with a different wavelength. Some of them are of a radiant nature, others are of a magnetic nature. Some of them are within the radar band frequency and we do not feel them. Thank God for that! If we felt all of these energies our world would be completely shattered. Our limitations are, in fact, for our protection. If our eyesight saw every detail we would be horrified; the carpet would appear as a jungle with millions of microbes in it, and so on. So the believer constantly sees Allah's perfection, and therefore is in constant glorification.

Continuing with the topic of wealth and poverty, there is a tradition from Imam Rida in which he says: "He who greets a poor Muslim differently from a rich Muslim will find that Allah will see him on the Day of Reckoning with anger." The Prophet said: "Look at those who are below you." Meaning, look at those who are worse off than you. It is another technique of bringing one to the state of gratitude.

In our modern materialistic society, we are taught to look up to those who have more than us. Consumerism is designed to escalate the agitation of those who are subjected to it in order to instill the desire for what is bigger, better and faster. Within the dynamics of desire-generation and its fulfilment there is a secret. The *kufr* or infidel system, just like the system of Islam, allows for the individual to attain satisfaction and, therefore, a state of momentary gratitude.

One cause of momentary happiness is the fulfilment of a desire. The less we desire, the more contentment we will possess and the happier we will be. If we were to be told that whatever we wanted in this world would be granted, we would experience a moment of happiness. The next moment, of course, something else would happen. The unbeliever also recognizes that a measure of happiness is achieved through the fulfilment of a desire. So the disbelievers fan the desires of their people through consumerism, making much of what is offered available. Efforts are made to make the products easily accessible through a plastic credit card so that for a split second the exhilaration of contentment is achieved.

The believer has reached the foundation or root of content- ment. He has gone beyond the little trick of achieving momentary happiness. Because Islam turns its people away from the banking, monetary system, it is a threat to the *kafir* system.

The believer is the biggest threat to the materialistic West because of what faith implies, but the majority of believers do not understand this. Reflect upon it. The consumer who chases after numerous different material objects during his day achieves only a split-second of contentment which the believer can achieve by sitting for fifty seconds and saying, 'Allah,' and emptying himself. The believer can then say to himself, 'No, I am discon- tented. I am not doing enough. I must see what I can do for my family, my fellow Muslims and humanity.' Because he is committed to doing his best, he is a slave — day in, day out, every second is accounted for.

> Nay! Man is evidence against himself,
> Though he puts forth his excuses.
>
> (75:14–15)

We are our own witnessers. Within each cell are chromosomes

upon which are written the entire story of our being and so we have our choice:

> Surely, we have shown him the way; he may be
> thankful or unthankful.
>
> (76:3)

Allah says to each soul before it is born into this world, "Am I not your Lord?" Either man is in a state of gratitude *shukr*, and therefore in contentment as befits his position as Allah's vicegerent *(khalifah)*, or in denial, covering it up, and making endless excuses. It is clear.

We are accountable to the One and Only. If we live by this reality with every breath, then there is hope for us as individuals and for humanity. Otherwise, Islam remains only sentimental, intellectual teachings. Those who know do, those who don't teach. Islam is about being. Whenever there is an Islamic Studies department, know that it is almost the end of Islam. Presently, there are more Islamic Studies departments in the *kufr* system than in the Muslim countries, but the Muslim countries will soon catch up because their Islam is fossilized — it is an official Islam, for ceremonies, superstitious, marriages and divorces.

People think that *wudu'* (ritual ablution) has to do with cleanliness, but actually it is a purely spiritual exercise performed in order to remember that nothing goes into our mouths unless it is completely in the way of Allah, and nothing comes out of our mouths that is poisonous, that is against anyone else. Likewise, *wudu'* reminds us that whatever we see, it is going to be for Allah's sake; and that we are not going to look at what is forbidden. Our right hand, the hand of right action, enjoins the good 'In the Name of Allah, the Beneficent, the Merciful', as is appropriate for the 'representative' of the Creator; while our left hand discards what is unworthy and forbids evil. *Wudu'* is a detailed inner ritual which presupposes our physical cleanliness.

We have to grasp the entire model of Islam which is devoted to Allah, the All-Encompassing. We cannot just take an aspect of Islam so that it becomes easy and comfortable. This is what 'official' Islam is today. In this used. The hadith quoted in this regard says that 'marriage is half the *din*, or way of Islam, so that you may pay attention to the other half which is more important'. The hadith, when it is mentioned as a whole unit, indicates that we should pay more attention to our spiritual dimension, but this cannot be done without first satisfying and containing our lower part. But the second half of this hadith is generally omitted because people do not want to hear it.

The purpose of existence is to know Allah. By practising only part of the *din* we will fall short of achieving our goal. Our lives will be without purpose if our priority is not to come to know Allah and prepare for the next life.

We may have a house, a wife, a car, and children, and then we will die. Is that acceptable to our intellect and sense of justice that, after we have done our utmost to learn how to live in this world and to know its purpose, that at the end there is only six feet of dust awaiting us? It can only be acceptable if we believe, perhaps blindly in the beginning, that there is only Allah and we have been put on earth to come to know the outer manifestations of what Allah has created of physical forms in order to know His Attributes and Names, and in our moments of inner silence become certain of the One and Only Reality Who encompasses all other realities emanating from the One Source.

Though the goal is beyond our comprehension, logic, and tongue, if it is not the purpose of our embracing Islam, then we are not embracing the right Islam. Islam is not about a certain ritual and the glorification of the Qur'an in its physical form. We have traditions of the Prophet which say that there will come a time when the Qur'an will be so revered that it is hardly read. This is our time. There is, increasingly, a tendency to put the Qur'an in velvet boxes.

The Commander of the Faithfull, 'Ali, says that we are the evident book. We must examine ourselves and the Islam that we are living. It is up to each of us to make ourselves accountable to our Creator. We are accountable to each other only for our outer conduct. We cannot judge others except by the outer crust of the *shari'ah* (divine law), in the hope that it will serve to preserve a vibrant inner core.

The men of Allah will be produced everywhere. The object of our Islam should be to create a situation from which men of Allah may emerge, and in which there are *walis* (friends of Allah) all around to remind us.

I once visited a cemetery in Morocco; there was so much light emanating from one of the graves that even a blind man could see it a hundred miles away. I asked whose grave it was, and was told that it was the grave of a man who died at an advanced age. At no time in his life was he known to have sat in a circle unless the talk was about Allah. This is what Islam is about, but it does not mean that we neglect our health and other fundamental aspects of our life. Actually, they are the first things we should set in order. Nor does it mean that we should first become rich and then start on a spiritual path. It does not work that way.

I have collected hadiths with the object of awakening people like us, living under difficult times. If we are not men of *tawhid*, aiming at unification with Allah, then we have missed the path. Our goal is to become people who see unity and cause and effect behind everything.

If we do not help to produce men of Allah, then we are not the hand of evolution, working on the path of Allah. In any case, Allah's path will prevail. Allah has promised that there will come a time when the entire world will be inhabited by men of Allah. The Qur'an says:

> Certainly we wrote in the Book after the reminder
> that (as for) the land, My righteous servants shall
> inherit it.
>
> (21:105)

As Muslims, we have to believe that a time of darkness will come in the world and that its opposite will also appear. Anything which moves beyond its boundary will turn into its opposite. Everything in existance — any plant, imagination, thought, is rooted in its opposite. The root of appreciating wealth lies in the knowledge of poverty. The root of appreciating health lies in experiencing illness. The times we are living in are so dark that

they will also turn to their opposite. It is the law of Allah and
Allah says about His last:

> And you shall not find any change in the course
> of Allah.   (33-62)

Everything has its secret in its opposite.

Now, everywhere throughout the world, there are hearts start-
ing to ask the right questions. The media, which is the cause of
all the oppression, will reverse itself. It is only a vehicle. Whatever
you put into it will come out.

So the time of the Mahdi is near. This is the good news. He
will come in a way in which we will understand. Maybe madmen
in some country will ignite one of the nuclear bombs, setting off
a chain reaction resulting in nuclear war. Where will it be safe?
Perhaps Sri Lanka or Bangladesh because nobody wants them.
The sooner we turn to our One and Only Friend and remain
with Him the better. The time we are living in is as we have
already indicated, the physical and spiritual corruption which
is now rampant throughout the world will decline. The land will
be overtaken by the men of Allah and the *khalifah* of Allah will
emerge. In the Qur'an Allah told this to the angels.

The Prophet who contained Adam's heart knew that at all
times Allah's justice prevails in spite of us. Our justice is within
Allah's creation just as our injustice is within His justice. The
believer sees the injustice of man, but He sees it within the
context of divine law.

Eventually, the justice of our earth will be unified with Allah's
justice. Allah's justice will prevail because there will be men of
Allah left on the earth.

The evolution which Allah promises is the coming of a time
when all men on earth will be *walis* (friends of Allah). This, not
Darwin's theory, is the description of the real evolution. Within
us is contained the meanings of all of the animals, without a
doubt. How can we understand the snake unless there is a snake
within us? And the time will come when those who are awakened
will be as light. The awakening of the intelligence began with
Adam.

We have come from a resurrected state, in which there was no discrimination. Adam, when Shaytan spoke to him, did not recognize his voice. He had only heard the voice of the Merciful One Who only spoke the Truth. A prophet is infallible. Question the Qur'an and find out the real meaning of this story. Adam did not make a mistake. When he heard another form of adoration which is called *shatana* in Arabic, meaning 'being far from Allah's prescribed path', which is the condition of Shaytan, he did not know that it was not to be followed. Allah had to cause Adam to leave the Garden in order for discrimination to arise.

We have no option but to increase in discrimination. We have to feed our faculty of reasoning. A time will come when everyone will be in almost pure consciousness, which is the meaning of *dhikr*, remembrance, awareness. Allah says in the Qur'an:

> There surely came over man a period of time when
> he was a thing not worth mentioning.
>
> (76:1)

Looking at the lowest and most obvious meaning of this *ayah*, we see that it says that there was a time when no one could mention us, no one could say any one of us would be born. Elevating our perception, we see that it also means there was certainly a time when we were in the *dhikr* of Allah. We were in the knowledge of Reality which is beyond time. A time will come when there will be full awakening for everyone.

May Allah bless all of you. May Allah give you the courage and the strength to move vigorously on the path of Islam. May Allah give you knowledge of the true faith in all its meanings. May Allah make us true brothers in Islam. May Allah fuse our hearts in faith.

3
Living Real Islam

Wherever I have been, I have noticed that there are new people who want to know Islam and the way to Allah; new people who are suffering from the way of unbelief or *kufr*. People only deny the existence of Allah because they lack the knowledge of *La ilaha illa'llah, Muhammadun Rasulu'llah* (There is no God but Allah, and Muhammad is His Prophet). At the same time, I have met a considerable number of Muslims whose Islam has become diluted or has not been confirmed by their actions — it has merely been inherited. The Qur'anic statement

> You are the best of the nations raised up for (the benefit of) men; you enjoin what is right and forbid the wrong and believe in Allah
>
> (3:110)

has not taken root in them.

There are many countries in the modern world where Islam has failed to take root as a complete way of life. Malaysia is a good example. A few hundred years ago some of the sultans embraced Islam and thereafter the people accepted the basic practices and rituals. But, for the most part, it has remained just another convenient way of keeping people at bay and maintaining the economic class structure. It is not the Islam of Muhammad. It is not the Islam described by the Prophet's words: "Poverty is my pride." Instead of establishing a dynamic Islam, they have introduced Islamic studies departments within the universities —what they have established is academic Islam.

In the last few years the demand for, and curiosity about, Islam has, to a great extent, coincided with the Islamic Revolution in Iran. People everywhere have been asking, 'How can a country live without either being under the control of America or Russia?' After fifty or sixty years of oppression, mediocrity, and *kufr*, the people in Iran are attempting to establish, in every respect, the true way of Islam. It will take some time for it to succeed. It will take time for the outer changes to enter into the heart so that the outer and the inner unify.

There have been an increasing number of people, especially
amongst the poor and the oppressed, who want to know: What
is the way of abandonment? What is the way of freedom? How
can man live on this earth, yet not belong to this earth? For a
few years we are imprisoned in our bodies on this earth but, in
essence, we do not belong to this earth. We all know we are
dying and that every step brings us closer to the death when
everyone will encounter the face of his Lord:

> With your Lord shall on that day be the place of
> rest.
>
> (75:12)

We all know, whether we like it or not, that this life is a short
journey from which we shall enter another zone of experience
which is beyond time, which is forever. The entity which is called
'I' will exist in the next world just as I have left it while living
on this earth. If I die as a good Muslim and a believer, this will
be the state of that entity in the beyond-time-zone.

Wherever we go, we find people who want to know the way
to submission. They want to know the way to Allah, to *"la ilaha
illa'llah"* (There is not god but Allah). We find that this step is
not difficult: even in the worst system of unbelief or *kufr* people
are ready to accept the fact that there is one Entity behind what
is happening. They are ready to accept that there is one hand
behind all things. Scientific research shows us, through the laws
of cause and effect, that the entirety of this existence is but one
fibre. Whatever we do affects the rest of existence. We are not
isolated. As the individual evolves, this knowledge gains a hold
within him and he begins to embrace the knowledge of *"la ilaha
illa'llah"*. But the acceptance of this knowledge is difficult. To
come to know the Prophet, his people, his companions and his
kinsmen, the *Ahl al-Bayt*, requires time and study. One has to
become acquainted with the Prophet's behaviour and special
qualities. How were he and his followers and household able to
be in this life and yet not of it? The Prophet said: "If you want
to look at a dead man walking, look at me." He also said: "Die
before you die." What do these statements mean? True Islam

only comes alive through the example of the Prophet and his
pure family and followers.

I have just come from Peshawar where I was with some of
the *mujahidin* (fighters for Allah). Two of them whom I met had
just come from the front the day before, having lost many of
their friends. You could feel that there was a different quality of
life amongst them. My experience of them was a proof that Islam
without *jihad* (struggle in the way of Allah) cannot exist. We
cannot take one part of Islam out of convenience and reject
another because it is uncomfortable. Islam is not about convenience but about Allah. It means living as though at any moment
you will see nothing other than Allah. The spiritual state of
excellence consists of acting as though you are seeing nothing
other than Allah. Although people unavoidably become attached
to certain aspects of Islam, the Qur'an or their teacher, a time
comes when the true seeker is weaned from that to which he is
attached, thereby enabling him to see nothing other than his
Createor. The teaching of Islam leads us to understand that.

Allah, Who is beyond time, knows what is going to be in time,
because time is contained in beyond-time. Time is an outer
manifestation of non-time. He is the First and the Last. You and
I experience time, and yet there is something in us that tells us
that we do not belong to this chain of events. The ignorant
kafirun, that is to say those who reject the truth, want to live
long. This is the extent of their understanding of *'ibadah* — the
worship and glorification of Allah. Allah says:

> Whatever is in the heavens and whatever is in the
> earth declares the glory of Allah.
>
> (64:1)

We glorify that Entity. The whole of creation glorifies Allah,
even the *kafir*. But we as Muslims do it in the correct way; we
unify our will with destiny, with Allah's will. And therefore, the
believer *(mu'min)* finds nothing other than the blessedness of
Allah's perfection even when everything around him is crumbl-
ing, because he remembers Allah's will and Allah's way. The
Qur'an, the Book of Discrimination, says:

> Allah is not unjust to them, but they are unjust to
> themselves.
>
> (3:117)

If we are in misery, if we are attacked, if we lose Afghanistan,
it is our fault. The blame for whatever occurs falls upon us. Allah
has given us, His representatives, the choice to be grateful or
disbelieving. Gratitude *(shukr)* is a condition of the heart. In
other words, gratitude should not only be on the tongue but in
the heart as well. What is the use of knowing the Qur'an by
heart and not applying it to our lives as a manual of existence
from minute to minute? You must be careful:

> Therefore read what is easy of the Qur'an.
>
> (73:20)

Every one of us can take what he can of it, joyfully, and move
on. The Qur'an says:

> Allah does not impose upon any soul a duty but
> to the extent of its ability.
>
> (2:286)

This means that Allah imposes a duty upon everyone to the
maximum of his or her ability. Allah, by forcing us to make
efforts, is teaching our hearts to be always turning, always grateful. He says:

> That you grieve not for what has escaped you, nor
> be exultant at what He has given you.
>
> (3:153)

The believer never looks back in sorrow or regrets what has
happened. If he does, it is only to attain the capacity to discriminate — to understand the underlying causes. Usually, loss and
failure is caused by distraction *(ghaflah)*, or by a lack of unity
between the intention and the action. If I have failed, it is because
I have not heard or properly understood the call to prayer which
includes the words *"Hayya 'ala'l-falah"*. *Falaha* implies to succeed
as well as to turn the earth upside down. If our hearts, or our

fields, which are this world, are not ploughed and made ready
for the Hereafter, there will be nothing for us but indignities.
We will have no right to claim the title Allah has given us.

The vicegerent or *khalifah* or Allah is he who, with every breath,
is aware and is willing. He is totally free of what is in this world
yet enslaved to his Creator. His heart turns freely within him.
Whenever he looks inward, he sees the incredible universe. Outwardly, he is a slave who cannot but follow the example or *sunnah*
of Muhammad. Outwardly he is sober, inwardly he is drunk.
Inwardly he is gratified at all times with knowledge, not because
he has had a good meal or he has taken a drug. The believer is,
at all times, prepared to unify his intention with his action.

The Islam of the East has been diluted. Even so, in agricultural
communities Allah's blessedness manifests outwardly through
the call to prayer *(adhan)* and going to the mosque. Rural Pakistan
is the land of hearts. A land in which *walis* are produced. But
walis (great men of Allah, inheritors of the Prophetic message)
do not come by inheritance. There is no guarantee that the
children of *walis* will also be *walis*. Allah says:

> He brings forth the living from the dead and brings
> forth the dead from the living.
>
> (30:19)

Though dead inwardly, Allah may bring us to life at any moment
in our life. Usually we are woken up through trouble that occurs
in our lives which causes us to conclude that nothing in this
world is worth struggling for — neither our wealth nor our
position. We have come into this world alone to be dumped
under six feet of dust. Our awakening usually occurs when we
are in distress and loss. Generally speaking, most of us wake up.

The Prophet said, "You are not a Muslim if there is one person
in your neighbourhood who goes to sleep hungry." There are
individuals in the world who have incomes of millions of dollars
which they spend on their petty luxuries while millions of people
amongst the Muslim communities have barely a meal each day.

Islam has become diluted by becoming an official Islam, paid
for by the government which provides each of the Imams with
an official *khutbah* (discourse or sermon). This is official Islam.

Vibrant Islam, found amongst the people, is what the system of unbelief is afraid of. Vibrant, green Islam, is an Islam which people want to know. There are no professional practitioners in Islam. Who were the professionals at the time of the Prophet, or at the time of the early Caliphs? The last leader of the army whom Muhammad appointed was Usama who was one of his youngest companions. Why did the Prophet not appoint one of the others who were much older? Who were the professionals and the graduates? I am not against Islamic colleges, but it is a reflection of the darkness of our times that because Islam is not deep within us, we have to create institutions to preserve it as a museum piece.

I cannot give you the good news without the bad news. The good news is that Islam is vibrant and growing in practically every land, from West Africa to Japan. We have been establishing small centres in which Islam flourishes. Into them we bring young people to learn about their *din*, the path of their religion, and then they are sent out into the world. In this way they see how unbelief creeps into people's lives, and they are then able to advise others on how to fight it.

There are billions of devils or Shaytans; every one of us has many of them. Every individual must be like a lion tamer of his Shaytan, for unless we watch him he will come out of his corner.

If we are Muslims, we must follow the entire way of Islam without omitting anything. It must not become a nice ceremonial thing, only for marriages, divorces, births and burials, carried out by a class of professionals who are only following the lure of a few rupees. Our heritage was the reverse; those who were teaching gave money in charity.

If you do not know Islamic history, go and find out. Beware of the fabrications of the Umayyad and the 'Abbasid dynasties. Simply because an historical account has come from the government does not mean that it is necessarily true. Yazid, one of the Umayyad rulers actually ransacked Mecca and tore down the Ka'bah.

If Islam is not based on a combination of intellect (*'aql*) and action (*'amal*), it is of no use. You will neither gain in this worldy life (*dunya*) nor in the Hereafter (*akhirah*). It is because of this principle that we find our 'Islamic' world in such a state of confusion. As far as the Hereafter is concerned, only Allah has knowledge of it. He says:

> And whoever is blind in this (world), he shall (also) be blind in the Hereafter and more erring from the way.
>
> (17:72)

If in this world, which is clumsy and obvious, we cannot be successful, how can we be successful in a situation which is so subtle such as the next world?

Depend on Allah, and Allah will bring you to the true path. He is not exclusive to a few *shaykhs* (teachers of the spiritual way) or *walis* (men considered friends of Allah because of their piety). Why don't you claim Allah? Allah is not the Preserver of the one or two. The Prophet was asked, "Who are the *Ahl al-Bayt* " (the People of the Household of the Prophet)? He said, "The *Ahl al-Taqwa* (People of fearful awareness)". *Taqwa* means precaution. How can you be cautious of something unless you know its nature? The nature of Reality manifests in the laws of creation. If we do wrong, we do wrong to ourselves because there is only one *nafs* (self). If we are insincere, we are insincere to ourselves. If we really want knowledge, it will come to us. The *walis* will come running after us. Otherwise, the situation is a superstitious nonsensical 'bless me' type. That is not Islam.

Inherited Islam is dangerous, because, although the people have had the blessedness of having been born and brought up in sweetness and with the constant invocation of Allah *(dhikr)*, they also have the tendency to disregard it. Familiarity breeds contempt. I have regained much of my Islamic heritage through those who have embraced Islam as adults because they ask questions that had never occurred to me. I took Islam for granted. They ask why the Muslim world is in misery. The answer is because their Islam is outward and not inward. It is very simple. Nine hundred million people profess Islam, but within this quantity of people there is very little quality. You, in this part of the world, are blessed with purity, with what has come to you from centuries of the original stream of Islam. If it is not fully revived on the basis of *tawhid* (unification), it will become diluted and lose its virility. So many great cultures went by the wayside because they became settled — they lost their ability to expand. It is for that reason I pray that Allah will give us some young people from here who have gained their Islam properly. We will send them out so that they may see that everywhere in the world people are seeking the true light of Islam.

All over the world people are asking for Islam but there are not enough teachers. I will not take a teacher unless he *is* Islam: he should embody the Book and the Sunnah; what he says should come from his heart and be confirmed by his intellect. I do not want preachers. There are enough of them in the forty-six so-called Muslim countries. Their boring propaganda comes to us through the media of television, radio, and so on. They are the people who love to be in the king's parlour. In our way, the king comes to the man of knowledge; the men of knowledge do not go to the king.

In spite of us, Islam will prevail in the world. This is the way of Allah. At best we are but His slaves. Allah promises in the Qur'an that this way, His light, *Nur Allah*, will prevail, and this will occur in man when he is fully awake. Allah says:

If you do good, you will do good for your own souls.

(17:7)

Both inwardly and outwardly, this life is *jihad* — a struggle in the way of Allah. We should be continually singing the one and only song of Allah: *"La ilaha illa'llah, Muhammadun Rasulu'llah"* (There is no god but Allah, and Muhammad is His Prophet), wherever we go. We have come to this town in order to change the direction of events. Recently, you have been losing your best people to the system of unbelief. We would like to bring back the best of them to help you, using the new outer technology of the West and the revived inner technology of the East. Simply importing outer technology will ruin us unless it is subservient to our knowledge of the way of Islam. If our moral values are not the dictating factors as to what and when this outer technology is used, it will be of no use to us. We are here with the hope that some people from this community will step forward. We hope that today's young *walis* or friends of Allah will be the people who are familiar with the language of unbelief, who not only know how it works but also understand the religion which they aim to revive. We visited some of the tribes in the North West Frontier. There you still see the purity of their hearts and the closeness of their tribes. But you can also see that this way of life is being eroded. Soon it will be a museum piece, unless they allow themselves to be led by *walis*. I gave them that message and that warning, and they all understood it; they were desperate and asked what they could do about it.

I was brought up in Karbala, a town built upon the spilled blood of Imam Husayn. The Karbala of the past is no longer. For that reason, we have to establish Karbala everywhere. That is the way of our Imams. There is a well-known *hadith* in which the Prophet said, "Husayn is from me and I am from Husayn." It is easy to understand the first part of the statement because Husayn was his offspring. But what did he mean when he said, "I am from him, from Husayn?" It means that Husayn is his message. The vital message of Islam would have died unless the blood of his grandson had been shed. People often ask: 'Why did he perish?' The answer is simple. Islam was becoming a dynastic rule. The followers of Mu'awiyyah were making it a hereditary kingdom, like others that had come before it. It was Husayn's blood that revived Islam.

Karbala is now just another modern city. In my youth this town had a population of over one hundred and fifty thousand people and yet almost everybody knew everybody else. People rarely moved house. I was brought up in a house that had been used by my family for one hundred and eighty years. We were originally from northern Iran. Like many other houses, our house had guest quarters and the guests were of all kinds — beggars, dervishes, rich and poor, often side by side. There were no hospitals, no prisons, no police. One could obtain all that one needed for this life or the next within one minute's walk. The Bazaars, the bakeries, the public baths and the mosques were all close at hand. But it is not like that any more. Along the streets the entire culture has collapsed. One cannot walk anywhere in the city any more, a car must be used — all in the name of 'modernization'. Is this progress? I would call it regress. This is what has ruined Islam, so-called 'modernization'. The medical knowledge of village doctors who were men of Allah has been replaced by the services of allopathic doctors who push drugs that are banned in the West as unsafe. This has occurred because we have been in a state of forgetfulness.

We were led by the worst amongst us. We did not demand to be led in this world by the spiritually enlightened. If the best amongst us spiritually are not going to lead us, if we are only going to put them in caves and in derelict places where we go to receive blessings, we are doomed. If our *walis* are not going to be amidst us leading us, day in, day out — something is wrong. If we do not want it, or they think we do not deserve it, in either case something is wrong.

I am not blaming any government whatsoever. In fact, because you are allowed to work, think, publish and revive the knowledge of Islam *('ilm)*, you have one of the best governments. In the situation you have here when you have any disagreement you can go back to the source and foundation, the Qur'an. If you go back to the way of Muhammad you will find out the truth. If there are still disagreements they will be so minor that they will be insignificant. You are very fortunate, but you have to take advantage of the opportunity, otherwise the caravan will pass you by. Pakistan can be a leading Muslim nation. There are four billion people on earth and Islam has to reach all of them, including the so-called Muslims. The Muslims are desperate to see people who are living their Islam. They do not want preachers. They want real Muslims. I pray that there will emerge from this country people who will sing, whose tongues will express what is in their hearts so that they may communicate the true knowledge to the rest of the world. Islam is the path or *din* of Allah. Allah pervades all and this earth belongs to Him. There are no territories. If we affirm that there are, we will fall into nationalism and racialism.

These are dark times. And in dark times, we must strike stones together in order to make sparks. It is the time when a one-eyed man is king in the country of the blind. People like myself, who have little knowledge, suddenly seem to be doing something which everybody talks about. With a little bit of insight, one seems to be the king. The Prophet said to his Companions: "If I tell you ten things and you forget one, you are in the Fire. A time will come when if a people remember but one of the ten they will be in the Garden." This is, possibly, our time. A few good deeds are very apparent in this time and age, but they must be sincere. Allah says:

> Do men think that they will be left alone (at ease)
> on saying, we believe, and will not be tried?
>
> (29:2)

It is a sign of Allah's love for us that He does not allow us to say something without meaning it. Even amongst rascals, good may come. Whatever we look for we will find, whether it be good or bad. Allah has instructed us in Surah Ali-'Imran:

> Enjoy what is right and forbid the wrong.
>
> (3:110)

Otherwise man is at a loss. There is no use in having faith unless it is accompanied by good actions. If that happens, then the command to do good and the prohibition of evil will make us righteous *(salih)* and the best of communities. Undoubtedly it is up to us. Allah has given us the freedom to do it. After all we have been born into that blessedness of Islam!

4

Remembrance of the Prophet

Any occasion to remember that which is worth remembering is worthwhile. And it is especially appropriate that we should remember the emissary or representative of Allah, the Prophet of the One and Only Reality. Muslims nowadays seem to have agreed to disagree, wherever they are. Let us hope that at least they will agree upon maintaining the memory and remembrance of the Prophet Muhammad, may the peace and blessings of Allah be upon him and his family. As you all know, there are two types of conditions we undergo in this life. One is transitory, made up of specific experiences and events that change. The other type is composed of situations that never change: they are the barometer upon which change is measured. This is the knowledge that we are born to acquire. This is the state of the Garden.

The meaning of the Garden is to be in a state of true submission, devotion and worship. This state cannot occur unless there is true abandonment, an experiential state of unity *(tawhid)*. The knowledge of how to acquire this experience is to be derived from the prophets, whom we seek to imitate and emulate.

With regard to the nature of prophethood, there is the possibility of confusion. Some people see a prophet as a divine transmitter of a divine message and others look upon him as a human being; and of course there are many variations in between these two extremes. On the one hand, he is accessible, he is human, he humours people, he sits with them, he shares with them and is one of them. On the other hand, he is a universal being who is totally committed and connected to Allah and inspired by Him. People would often take liberties because of this intimacy. Within the prophetic situation there are these two aspects. The Prophet had that unchangeable connection with Allah which enabled him to reveal laws that have never changed and will never change, but he was also subject to change. Every day was a different day for him, every moment a fresh moment. For this reason some of us try to preserve that heritage, knowledge, personality, or state of being. We are afraid of changes, and attempt to fossilize the dynamism of life for fear of bringing in some

aberration or innovation. And yet every moment of his life the
blessed Prophet Muhammad was fresh and totally dynamic;
biologically also, moving in time from childhood to old age to
the experience of death and back to freedom from the material
world. Yet constantly, at all times, he was aware of the non-time.
Allah encompasses time, is beyond time and His own manifestations, and His signs are everything which we can experience.⌐

At the height of the biological condition is the human being
and at the lowest end is the stone, which also has its life, its
dynamism. We should remember the reality of this every moment
of our lives.

Gatherings are only to accentuate, to punctuate, so to speak,
the continuous remembrance which true, living and fully
awakened human beings can never forget. How can we forget
the fact that we are breathing? How can we forget the fact that
we are getting closer to the experience of death? How can we
forget that we have come as a clot, and will end up under six
feet of dust? How can any individual in his right mind forget
this incredible event? There is within him an ego that can destroy
him, but there is also within him the possibility of maintaining
an open heart that can liberate him. How can anybody forget
these possibilities? We are caught in a body that must be
nourished, sustained, maintained, and yet, at the same time, we
long to be eternal. We therefore wish that whatever is worthwhile,
any relationship or state of well-being, would last forever.

We are trapped in this world in order to be prepared for the
final awakening, in order to be tuned and made fully available
for a state of pure life — a state of existence that is pure in its
totality and its eternity.

Remembrance of the Prophet is remembrance of the interspace
between an eternal Reality that is not subject to time, and a
mortal, human, material situation which has its ups and downs,
friendships and enmities, loves and hates, and so forth. All of
this exists so that we may see the Oneness that encompasses
duality.

Remembrance of the Prophet is to remember the truth that
he revealed. There is a beautiful line of poetry: 'The Prophet
himself lies behind the curtain of Karbala.' He said, 'Husayn is

from me and I am from Husayn.' If it were not for Husayn the knowledge of the Prophet would have been lost. The question of who was going to lead the Muslim community after the Prophet's death was not a question of hereditary rights, rather it was a question of who was the best man to emerge spiritually, naturally, so that the weaker human beings could learn from him, if they wished, because, as He says in His Qur'an,

> Allah does not change a people unless they change
> their own condition.
>
> (13:11)

The Creator's ultimate love for His creatures is His gift of the choice of submission or rebellion. Man is given the chance to reach a point of non-choice, which in reality is the only choice, namely total and utter submission.

This way is for the open-hearted, for those who are by nature uncomplex, who are fortunate to be in a state of devotion. For others who need to nurture the intellect and combine emotions with reasoning, the opportunity is also open if action is taken after discrimination. The people of intellect must serve, otherwise, the result is confusion and hypocrisy, for instead of following the best amongst people in a spiritual sense, they will follow those who are best in worldly or material terms. Thus, the spiritual aspect is separated from the material aspect, which fosters hypocrisy.

If we are not living as if the Prophet is with us, next door to us, then no matter how much we air our emotions and our love for him, our real situation will not change. No matter how much we recite the Qur'an and appear to be in obedience, if our devotion is not translated into a living reality from which we derive continuing benefit and nourishment, we will remain Muslims in name only. This is the situation of mankind and it has been so since time immemorial.

Man is given the choice of being tuned with love, reverence, understanding, and reason to the Prophet. By this means he may ignite the light of Muhammad in his own heart to guide his actions towards a glorious destiny, from the glorious beginning of the "Be and it is" to the liberation of physical death, which is the beginning of a new life. If we do not choose to implement the prophetic pattern, then we may choose to be simply superficial Muslims, congratulating ourselves every time someone embraces Islam.

Remembrance of the Prophet can be used to ignite either the faculty of reasoning or the heart in order to obtain knowledge, the foundation of light, from that Perfect Being who was a reflector of the Divine Reality amongst evolving creatures. That knowledge must be taken, digested, utilized and unified with. But this is what is so often missing. Many of us have love, kindness and remembrance, but this is not enough if it is not backed by knowledge, the knowledge of the proper boundaries and courtesies by which one should live both inwardly and outwardly, the knowledge that will permit us to practise being in the garden in this life before entering the Garden in the next. Even if no garden were to exist afterwards, at least one would have done something here; lived a full, joyous life, an uncompromising life as far as the truth is concerned, a life of freedom and abandonment.

We who profess to love the blessed Prophet are bound by the need to acquire the knowledge which we have just mentioned, unifying with it, being it. Without it, there will continue to be gatherings without action, as has been the case for the last 500–600 years: there will be more and more remembrance of Imam Husayn, yet we will become further and further removed from the real battlefield of Karbala, inwardly and outwardly. The inward and the outward must be united. What is the use of censuring our neighbour if our own home is not in order? It is hypocrisy.

Our first concern is our immediate environment, then our relatives, our families, our neighbours, our cities, our societies, and finally the whole of mankind. There is a hierarchical order which establishes a code of conduct for everything. It would be out of order to preach to outsiders without having first put our own house in order. And we cannot begin to do this without adhering to the Muhammadi way of creation, the pattern of complete human development based upon the unchangeable truth.

The Muhammadi pattern was fully elaborated by the twelve

Imams of the Prophet's house who followed him as visible guides for the span of three hundred years after his death. They had the same light of the Muhammadi truth, the same inner reality. Their outwardness was different, each according to the necessities of his time. Imam Hasan abandoned his army while Imam Husayn fought to the death. Imam Hasan did not capitulate, rather, through a precise knowledge of the weakness of the people he recognized the futility of making a stand at that point in time. Imam Husayn, on the other hand, though he had only a few followers, knew that a stand had to be made so that the Muhammadi light would not be extinguished. In their inner reality or inner awakening Imam Hasan and Imam Husayn were the same, even though their actions seem to us completely different. The truth never changes, but the way it manifests makes it appear to change. This is the way of Allah for His creation. The theatre looks different every moment, every breath is fresh, yet a breath is a breath; it inhales purity and exhales impurity.

If our remembrance of the Prophet Muhammad does not lead us to the awakening of his light, which is based on knowledge, then we have missed the point, we have missed the opportunity, a moment in which our heart could have awakened, leading us to freedom here and now, not hereafter. If this awakening does not occur here, how can it occur there? Now it is in our hands, we seem to have been given that choice, although limited, within Allah's decree. We have a certain measure of choice wihtin what He has decreed. That decree is contained in His knowledge and His knowledge is His business only. The knowledge that we are given is our business. We must strive to acquire it, learn, apply and unify with it. We are then accountable for it.

Let us share a few of our prophetic traditions, for unless these traditions become real we will have inherited a set of values that are twisted to suit social and national circumstances. An indication of our condition today may be reflected in the reply of Imam ʿAli to the question of why he did not claim his right as the leader of the Muslims after the Prophet's death. He said: "Give me forty men... ." This means that even at that time there were not forty real beings. So think of us in this time. On the other hand, Allah says in the Qur'an:

I do not take from you a sign unless I replace it
with something better.

(8:70)

So although our time is terrible outwardly, the world is more
closely knit in many ways. Materialism in its positive aspect is
providing the means for wider dispersal of knowledge. People
suddenly find themselves gathered together from different parts
of the world, with different backgrounds, sharing the same thing.
This phenomenon is happening more and more all over the world.

We are in this world now, so we must revive that which stands
the test of time and apply it to the present rather than be
superstitious and romantic about previous ways of living. Imam
Ja'far as-Sadiq said: "Do not expect your children to be like you,
because they were born in a different time." What he meant was
that their situations would be different, not their inner core.
Times and conditions will change but the truth will not change,
nor will the love for those who expound the truth. There will
always be those who love the Prophet and the people of Allah,
and there will always be those who hate them. The polarization
of truth and falsehood will not change. One cannot prohibit
wrong without commanding what is correct. This is a fact that
cannot be altered. But the way to call to what is correct may be
different now than it was thirty or forty years ago. We are dealing
with different circumstances which require a different language
acceptable to this time.

Returning to our intention to share a few prophetic traditions,
the Prophet said: "Allah loves excessive remembrance. Whoever
remembers Allah much will be free from the Fire and free from
hypocrisy." The way to begin remembering Reality is to negate
non-reality. The statement of unification "There is no god but
Allah" begins with negation of everything other than Reality.
We begin by saying, "This way is not acceptable, arrogance,
idolatry, and avarice are not acceptable." in order to love Allah
one must begin without even formally acknowledging His name.

The meaning of this tradition is that he who remembers Allah
is good in every state, no matter where he is, how he is, because
he is remembering that Reality which is beyond time. We, as
in-time beings, are subject to the laws of time, and we constantly

resent it because we want permanency, we want to be liberated from limitations. But Allah is the Limitless, and He contains all that is limited.

The Prophet equates the fire with hypocrisy because both are utterly destructive forces, whereas the way of Islam is unification, the seen and the unseen, this life and the next. We recognize goodness even if what comes to us is normally experientially recognized as bad. Unification is based on seeing the One hand behind what appears to be diversity. This point is beautifully expressed in the following *hadith*. A bedouin came to the Prophet and said: "Teach me some of the strange or higher forms of knowledge." The Prophet replied: "What have you done concerning the head of knowledge, that you have come to its unusual aspects?" The Prophet's reply meant, "Are you asking about the unusual because you have already grasped the usual?" The man then asked: "What is the head of knowledge?" The Prophet said: "To know Allah truthfully as He deserves to be known." This tradition has come from many sources, one of which is Ibn 'Abbas. The man again asked: "What is it to know Allah truthfully as He deserves to be known." The Prophet answered: "That you know Him without likening or comparing Him, for there is nothing like Him." There is nothing like Him because He is the One, the Only, and the Eternal. He is not something to exemplify something else. He is a Reality that is the cause of all other realities. Every other reality is its proof. He is His own proof. Imam 'Ali said: "If there was any other than Him, we would have had his messengers." We have had thousands of messengers, all from the same source, singing the same song, repeating the same thing. Linguistically and culturally different, from different places and times, yet alluding to the same Reality which they discovered within themselves. The Prophet continued teaching this ignorant bedouin: "Surely He is One, One without number, the Outward, the Inward." He is evident yet He is hidden. He is the first without firstness and He is the last without lastness. Allah is beyond time. Time has emanated from Him — how, we don't know. Even if we discover the biological 'hows' of the way we were created, it wouldn't give us the whole story. It is only an excuse that we say a father and a mother, an embryo.

How? Actually, we do not know. It is the "Be" of the "Be and it is." We can only allude to it for we are caught in it. We want freedom, trust, love, sincerity, loyalty, we want all these things which are already ingrained in us at a subgenetic level. The Prophet continued, "...the First, and the Last. There is none equal to Him, and that is as He deserves to be known." There is none equal to Him because there is one Reality, and that Reality is unique. We are not unique, we are repetitive. There is nothing different about any one of us as human beings. We are the same consciousness, from one self, appearing in pairs as man and woman. To know Allah in this way is to do justice to Reality.

Remembrance of the blessed Prophet is remembrance of Allah. The way to Allah is the way of the light of Muhammad, which is alluded to as having been created before the rest of creation.

Light is a subtle reality that unveils other realities. By it one sees the contours of physical realities. "Allah is the light of the heavens and the earth." Allah Himself is not light, light emanates from Him. What we see in the heavens and the earth is His light which allows us to witness reality outside and inside us. Thus we become our own witnessers.

> Nay! Man is evidence against himself,
> Though he puts forth his excuses.
>
> (75:14–15)

We know our own state. We know how real we are. Much of our preaching is not heeded because it is useless and usually very boring. Watch some of these pompous 'mullahs' and other people who appear now and then — they bore people to death. We have separated our Islam, we have made it a profession. Islam must be everybody's profession, to profess the truth that we have come to die, to know and to learn how to abandon ourselves, to recognize that abandonment does not occur with the head only, it must also be with the heart.

The love of the blessed Prophet could unify us, but it may not be enough for all of us. Some of us are devotionally inclined and that is enough for them — such people are fortunate. Others must find the reason for everything and reach to the innermost.

Unless they do that, they still remain doubtful and have no certainty, and therefore, their freedom is incomplete. This too is the Muhammadi way. The door to the Muhammadi way is 'Ali because he has made the way accessible. He is a door such that when you are standing in it you do not see the frame. Because the Prophet had that divine element in him, people were sometimes puzzled. 'Ali was not a prophet, he therefore made the knowledge more human and more fully available.

Thus our love for the Prophet's Household is not dogma. It is a courtesy, an easy way that gives us quick access to the companionship of the Prophet. We are born in a hurry, so let us hurry towards that presence, that reality, that light, that way of life, rather than blame somebody else such as a politician or a government. Nobody is going to do it for us.

In a sacred tradition from Allah, the Prophet said: "The angel Gabriel came to me and said, 'Oh Ahmad, Islam is ten divisions, and he who has no share in any of them has lost. The first share is to bear witness that there is no god but Allah.'" There are, as you know, many different degrees of witnessing. One of them is simply saying the words and not knowing the real meaning of what has been said. Another degree is experiential witnessing that there is no way out except submission to Allah, Glory be to Him. The whole affair begins with the verbal acknowledgement. One becomes a witnesser of the truth and the degree of one's recognition and knowledge of the truth. After "There is no god but Allah" comes "Muhammad is the Messenger of Allah." There is no god but Allah is generally easy. Anybody who is intelligent will recognize that there is no reality except One Reality. "Muhammad is the Mesenger of Allah" is more difficult, because suddenly one sees a human form who is a divine manifestation, a cosmic being, and yet he is accessible. So people become familiar and abuse him, forgetting the truth behind him.

"...And the second (division) is prayer and its purification." Prayer is abandonment, connectedness, effacing the profile of the self. First, reality is acknowledged in a dual form, by recitation of the Qur'an in a standing position. Then, upon the awakening of intelligence, one bows in submission. And finally there is prostration which is the effacing of the self. These are the pillars of the prayer. If any of them are missed, the prayer is invalid. And of course the door to the prayer is the ritual washing beforehand.

"...The third division is to pay the lawful tax, and it is an innate aspect of character." The root of the word for the alms tax *(zakat)* also means increase, purification, and giving away. We must give, because what we have is not really ours. How did we acquire what we have? Everything that we possess is a temporary loan from Allah. Giving is ingrained in us because we are takers. If one wants closeness to the Giver, then one must emulate Him. There are hierarchies of giving: to give what is needed, to give more than what is needed, to give before it is asked for. These are all attributes of Allah, but man can do something more; he can give what he himself needs. Allah has no needs so He does not do that. One of our Imams was asked the secret of the alms tax *(zakat)* which is the equivalent of two and a half per cent of one's yearly savings and capital after allowing for expenses. He said that the natural law of Allah's creation was that out of every thousand people there are twenty-five who are incapable of earning and taking care of themselves. This tax is to purify us, to make us become the conduit for an unbeginning, unending ocean of blessedness.

"...The fourth (division) is fasting, and it is the Garden." Expansion is not possible unless there is contraction. The mercy of wordly situations is not recognizable without the mercy of self-containment, and it is a hidden garden, the garden of inner awareness. There are, of course, degrees of fasting. One degree is the fast of the stomach only. Another is the fast of the tongue and all the senses, and still another degree is when the heart does not move away from the recognition of Allah.

"...The fifth division is the pilgrimage." The word for pilgrimage in Arabic is *hajj*, derived from the verb meaning 'to convince'. A derivational form means 'evidence, reason', thus it is related to witnessing. During the pilgrimage we perform acts that encapsulate the entire life cycle. We are running from Safa to Marwah, from one rock mound in a barren nowhereness to another. We walk slowly and we walk fast. This is also what we do when we are trying to catch the 100 rupees, or the bus or the train or whatever — we run after it. We go around the Ka'bah as we go around our own hearts. When we pray, we strive to face the Ka'bah for it is the *Qiblah*. However, it is not recommended to pray inside the Ka'bah, because if you pray to one wall, it necessitates turning one's back to the other walls. During the pilgrimage the poor and the rich are all together, gathered on the plain of 'Arafah. The word *'arafah* is derived from the word which means to 'know, acknowledge, recognize'. To know what? There is nothing but this vast desert. Where does one look?

> Wherever you turn there is Allah.
>
> (2:115)

But is this our reality upon experiencing the *hajj*? Nowadays those who wish to save their health must go by helicopter instead of on the ground because everybody is sprayed with D.D.T. This is what we have made the *hajj*. Imam Zayn al-'Abidin, upon him be peace, one day was approached by a man who was very pleased to see so many people performing the pilgrimage. The man said: "What a wonderful *hajj* it is this year." The Imam turned to him and said: "There are three people making *hajj* this year, me, my camel and one man from Basrah." We have greater and greater quantity, and lesser quality.

"...And the sixth division is battle *(jihad),* and it is honour and high rank." *Jihad* is of two dimensions: one dimension is fighting oppression and the other is fighting the inordinate desires of the self. The second dimension is higher than the first and should precede the first. The word *jihad* comes from the Arabic word meaning to expend energy and from it comes the word *mujtahid:* he who expends his energy in the pursuit of knowledge, to unify with the source from which knowledge comes.

"...And the seventh division of Islam is to enjoin goodness and correct action. It is called loyalty." Allah has been so generous to us in granting us awareness, senses, and powers of discrimination. Therefore to be loyal is to do the best we can, not only for ourselves, and those close to us, but for anyone.

"...And the eighth division is to prohibit what is disagreeable, and it is a proof." Have we said what deserves to be said when conditions around us are not acceptable? If we do not speak the truth, the unacceptable situation will affect us also. Why are we in a situation where we cannot speak the truth? Who told us to remain there? When affliction comes, it will cover everyone, including those who know. Allah's way is total. But the man of knowledge and faith at least knows why it is occurring, that is his consolation. The Prophet, may the peace and blessings of Allah be upon him and his family, lost his teeth when he was hit by an arrow because people disobeyed his commands during the battle of Uhud. He was not spared. Why should he be spared? In his total abandonment, in his unitive state, the loss of his teeth was immaterial. He only saw Allah behind all of those scenes to which we give so much importance. That being the case, what chance do we have?

"...And the ninth division is community spirit." Islam cannot exist unless there is a group of people living together and sharing. We cannot talk about such a phenomenon today. It does not exist. The Prophet said: "He is not a Muslim who sleeps and has a neighbour in his village who is hungry." This means one of two things: either many of us are not Muslims, or many of us have left Islam, because there are many poor Muslims whom we are not reaching. The issue is not about food, it is about reaching a point of equilibrium through the use of our intellect. The animals go out, hunt or graze and are alright. We must also find a way of providing for ourselves in a balanced way. It is Allah's way to cause our faculty of intellect, reasoning and discrimination to grow and evolve. So the community spirit is important, because it exists in the realm of duality, and duality is the medium for evaluation and growth. Regarding this Allah said in a well-known hadith:

> I was a hidden treasure and I wanted to be known,
> so I created the world.

Adam, upon him be peace, had complete knowledge resulting from discrimination before the occurrence of this waveband called Shaytan.

"...And the tenth division is obedience, and it is familiarity." How can we obey unless we know intuitively, intimately, that it is the right thing to do? None of us wants anything other than the best for himself: we are automatically programmed. If we follow that programme, then we follow the way for which we have been created, the way which will liberate us. We want to obey the truth, but the truth has to be awakened in us. Something, however, is needed from the outside to reflect the inner reality, so that we see the truth beyond time, beyond space, beyond the individual bounds, so that we talk about mankind and humanity as oneness. As it is now, the 4.7 billion people on earth are, for the most part, fragmented because of hypocrisy and division, because we do not see the one hand behind diversity. Thus the Prophet tells us that the tenth share of Islam is to obey, but obedience will not occur unless we test it. Sometimes that test can be futile, that is why we have to be careful. If we transgress too far the situation may become irreparable. If somebody jumps from a high building, there is no use in him saying, 'Pray for me'; it is too late. The way of Allah is that the law of gravity will not simply stop because of us. Physical laws prevail in this physical existence. For example, if there is excessive noise, or disturbance, we will not be able to communicate — that disturbance takes over because of its physicality. If we were all desperately hungry, we would not be able to sit and share something which is subtle. The blessed Prophet called together his tribesmen and fed them first before he started saying anything. First the belly must be subdued, then the emotions and passions harmonized, then silence is possible. From silence comes the truth.

Each one of us who loves the Prophet will be in a different state at each moment. That condition is creativity without deviating from the truth. Every circumstance requires its own approach. The time we live in is different from times before. The knowledge we need must be relevant for our age. There is a book of traditions called *Al - Kafi*, which means 'that which is sufficient', so named because at that time it was sufficient. How many of us have read *Al - Kafi* from cover to cover? Look at us now, we are so distracted that such an endeavour is for most of us impossible. We need to be given our knowledge, our Muhammadi Light, packaged in a way that is useable and assimilatable.

Look at the centres from where Islam spread in India, from

the *Ahl al-Bayt*, from Shaykh Mu'inaddin Chishti, from Nizamaddin Awliya, and from others. There is nothing but darkness in these places now. Not only is there a lack of inner light but even the outer electric lights are frequently going off. What is left? In Ajmeer Sharif, four hundred beggars are fed every night and almost everyone is a beggar. We spent two days there and did not see a single person reading the Qur'an. No teaching, no knowledge, because the knowledge is not packaged for our time. There is not one single book of the traditions or the teachings of the Prophet's Household that you and I can read with clarity and ease. There is not one book that gives us our history in the true light so that we do not become proud of certain events that we should be ashamed of. This is the age of food processors and refrigerators. We have achieved all this for our bellies, but we have not done it for our hearts and our souls. We have prepared ourselves in material, but not in spiritual, terms. Therefore, outwardly we are heavy and inwardly we are as light as a feather. Every little event knocks us off balance. Remembrance of the Prophet's steadfastness in the face of difficulty will lead us to yearn for the same knowledge, presented in a way that we can immediately utilize. We cannot sit for twenty years in a theological school *(madrasah)*. Very few people are fortunate enough to do that. The need of our age is so urgent that the truth will be unveiled quicker and quicker. Our own children can easily outstrip us if we at least show them what to avoid. In a way, we have been brainwashed by the conditions of our time. We may blame it on colonialism or whatever, but in fact colonialism is from within us. If we were strong enough we would have worked to spread our knowledge, love and generosity to all mankind. But because we were so small and feeble, we allowed others who were more single-minded, who knew what they wanted, to come and rob us. And we deserved it.

Thus we have nobody to blame but ourselves. Allah willing, this will give us the desire to live as though the Prophet is consoling us, communicating with us, guiding us, and giving us occasional reassurances. May Allah forgive us all because He is the All-Forgiver, and He stands by His word because He says:

> I have written upon Myself (decreed) Mercy.
>
> (6:12)

He has signed His part of the contract, now it is up to us to sign our part. May the peace and blessings of Allah be upon Muhammad and his family.

5

Freedom from the Chain of Desires

Although I have occasionally toured the Muslim countries, most of my work and my heart has been drawn to those who have not had the opportunity of knowing the true essence of Islam, rather, they have simply been exposed to so-called Muslims, and they have often been put off by the experience. I will never forget that during my first year in America when we arranged for twelve Americans to go on *hajj*,, each of them told me upon their return that if they had previously (before becoming Muslims) been on *hajj* and seen the so-called Muslims, they would never have embraced Islam. I am telling you the truth. Most of our efforts have been directed towards those unfortunate people who have not had the opportunity, like ourselves, of having inherited something that we may call Islamic behaviour and values. Having inherited a set of values, a courtesy, from whoever it may have been, perhaps our parents or grandparents, many beneficial qualities are still to be found among us although we may be ashamed of the behaviour of the Muslim community as a whole. Our collective or public behaviour leaves much to be desired; whereas our private behaviour still contains many of the traditional Islamic values. After all, after one thousand four hundred years of being exposed to Islam, something must remain.

Islam is about public duties and responsibilities, it is about the Ummah — the Muslim community; it is about the total illumination of mankind. For, the Prophet was sent as a mercy to all the world *(Rahmat lil-'alamin)*; it is not only confined to us and our families. Islam is total ecology, it is the path of unification, unifying us, our neighbourhood, our society, our country, mankind, and the whole cosmos.

Islam must move outward and expand, otherwise it will shrink. As we all know, there is no static situation, be it moral, economic, military or otherwise. If we are not expanding we are contracting, and generally speaking, these two cycles go hand in hand. Life is itself expanding and the cosmos itself is exploding. Man himself grows in size until he reaches a point where the process is reversed. The cosmos and man will collapse back to where they have come from. As far as man's spirit is concerned, it returns to the unknown, back to reality, back to Allah; and as far as his body is concerned, it becomes a bundle of minerals and organic matter which is recycled over and over again. I would like to share with you my heart-felt desire to see the revitalization of the Islam that has already come to us. We are not going to come up with anything new, nor to add to what Allah has already given us after thousands of years, after one hundred and twenty-four thousand Prophets have come and made Islam available and useable in all circumstances and at all times. The only thing we can do is take cognizance of the people's changing needs. In this age we need an Islam that is contemporary, available, as-similatable, useable, so that we can live it rather than talk about it. If we are talking about Islam we are not living it. Once we have separated Islamic studies or the study of the Qur'an from our day-to-day lives, we have abandoned *tawhid*, the principle of unification.

There was a man who once came to Imam Ja'far as-Sadiq and told him: "I have been afflicted with the desire for this world." The Imam asked, "What do you mean?" The man said, "Because I work hard and I am interested in my earnings." So the Imam asked him, "But what are you doing with your earnings?" The man replied, "I am providing for my family, my relatives and the people around me so that their lives are congenial and orderly and so that they are thereby better able to attend to their worship and inner awakening." The Imam said, "This is not the desire for this world, you are working for the Hereafter."

Outer connection and slavehood must be linked with inner abandonment. We cannot have one without the other. Inwardly, we should feel free and unattached; while outwardly, we are attached to our society, community, family, and our responsibilities. These two things go hand-in-hand.

Concerning *zuhd*, which means 'renunciation', 'abstinence', or 'asceticism', Imam 'Ali said: "*Zuhd* does not mean that you should not own anything, it means that nothing should own you." To have something and not be owned by it is far more difficult, and it is for this reason that the weaker among us take off to the mountains or say, 'We don't want anything.' They know they can become attached.

I will never forget a story which I was told years ago, when I used to spend a lot of time in India, of a genuine *zahid* who took off to the mountains with only one *doti*, only one piece of cloth, wrapped around him. But it was not long before he felt that he needed another *doti* because he needed another one to wear while he washed the first. So he told the people in the village that he needed one more piece of cloth. Knowing that he was a pious man, they gave it to him, and with his two pieces he once again ascended the mountain. After a time he discovered that, as he was meditating, a mouse would come and drag his extra cloth away. He didn't want to kill the mouse, only to frighten it. He could not leave his meditation and prayers all the time just to run after a mouse. So he descended to the village and told the people that he wanted a cat. Soon after having taken the cat, he realized that it could not live like him, eating a few berries and fruits; there were not enough mice for it to feed on and it needed milk. So after a few weeks he returned to the village and asked for some milk. The people knew it was not for him because he did not care for anything. But soon the milk was finished. He became worried because he was now going up and down the precarious, stony paths to the village for milk. To eliminate the problem of fetching milk, he took a little cow which would provide milk for the cat. Now he found himself milking the cow to care for the cat; 'There are so many poor people,' he said to himself, 'I'll ask some poor beggar from the village to come and milk the cow for the cat's sake.' A poor fellow, almost dead, living by a mosque, was brought up the mountain. After two or three weeks of the mountain air and lots of good milk he became healthy. The man then told the *zahid*, "Look, its alright for you, but I want a wife!" The *zahid* thought to himself, 'He's quite right, I can't deprive him of companionship.' So, to cut a long story short, after two months the whole village moved up the mountain.

There is no end to the materialistic chain of desire. First we want a better house, then we want to improve it with a bigger door, a refrigerator, a driveway, one car, two cars, three cars. In other words, we don't know when enough is enough. Even if we were earning million of rupees, we would consider ourselves to be average. If we earn five hundred rupees, it is the same. It is a strange phenomenon that we consider ourselves at the centre of the world at all times, and essentially we are at the centre of our own experiential worlds. Inwardly, in a meaning sense, we are at the centre of the cosmos. The point that I wish to make is that our Islamic heritage now only needs to be revived. Allah has given the procedure to us in such a way that it can be separated from the culture into which it was received. Islam is not based on a culture of camels. It was bestowed on the Arab culture but it can work among the Eskimos as well. It can work anywhere at any time and it is provable. We do not have to go to Arabia to be a real Muslim. Rather, it needs to be explained and demonstrated that Islam is better than any other system — and this as yet has not been done. It is not our intention to point the blame at anyone. The problem that faces us cannot be solved in this manner.

Right now our Islam is not in fashion. We assume that it is the fault of the jurists, or the book of hadiths, but *we* are to blame. The scholars have done their best. What is the point of blaming them? It is not going to benefit us.

I have noticed in our Islamic history that there have been specific locations in which the atmosphere was so wonderful that people seeking knowledge would become attached to those places. In Karbala, when I was a young boy, people came there from all over the world, even from such places as Tibet. I remember their eyes and faces. No sooner had they come than they found a garden of knowledge, so lush, so incredible. Most of them never returned to their old lives, instead they remained there until they died. Now, you may say that they were selfish, but I say they were looking after their souls. When a man who was appointed as governor asked Imam 'Ali for his final advice, the Imam said, "Just save your soul." If we are safe and our conduct, our whole way of life, is correct, then everything else is correct. Ultimately, this is our responsibility. Once we have accomplished this, our responsibility includes others. The knowledge that will save our souls is attained through service to others.

Recently in England I had the opportunity of keeping the company of a great man from North Africa, one of the great hidden masters. While I was with him I said, "I have had my fill of people, all they are is trouble. I would really like to spend more time by myself for my own nourishment." He replied, "But don't forget arrival is by them and, at the same time, affliction is through them." One's involvement with people is analogous to one's use of electricity. If we know how to use the power which is available and show the proper courtesy towards it, both us and those around us will benefit. But, if our courtesy towards it is not correct, we will harm ourselves and others.

One of the courtesies that is to be practised in one's involvement with others is 'speaking to the people according to their understanding'. 'Man is an enemy of what he does not know,' so if we are to relay the message of Islam properly we must be in contact with the people. Allah is the ultimate connector and His method is the way of unification. But occasionally the gulf seems so wide that we see nothing other than distraction and destruction — as we see nowadays in so many of our so-called Muslim communities. We follow the fashion and tradition and superficialities of Islam, but, in reality, it is only skin-deep for we do not benefit from the joy of faith and the freedom of surrender to the One and Only Creator from Whom we have come, by Whose mercy we are breathing and to Whom we are returning whether we know it or not. My task is to offer a diagnosis of our malaise. One problem is that, for the modern man who wants to know the Muhammadi way, Islam is not available in a manner which is usable or easily assimilatable. Nowadays, we are all used to easier ways of preparing foods. But the spiritual knowledge which provides food for our souls is not being made available in a manner that is usable. If we have to dig it up from the field, wash it, then cut it up; by the time we can eat it, we will have almost reached the grave.

I will give you some specific examples of what I am referring to. There is not one Qur'an with a simple, succinct yet deep commentary on the outward and inward meanings that can be read easily. It does not exist in Arabic, Farsi, Urdu, English or any other language. There are a number of magnificent *tafsirs*, the last one of which I am extremely fond of is by Ayatullah Tabataba'i of Qum, in twenty volumes. But it is impossible to read it from cover to cover. Even I, who have the time, have not read it in that way. The Muslims of the jet age need a brief commentary on the Qur'an which will instantly give them the balanced view — the historical basis of the *ayah* as well as its contemporary meaning. This easily accessible *tafsir* should also give the abrogating and abrogated *ayats*. The scholar, on the other hand, needs all the *tafsirs* and there are seven or eight without which he cannot do.

Along with the Qur'an we need hadiths. The Prophetic traditions are essential because they offer a model of how the word of Allah can be translated into the human situation. There are a great many collections from the Sunni sources and several great collections from the school of the *Ahl al-Bayt* such as *Al-Kafi, Wasa'il Shi'ah* and several others. But how many *Wasa'il Shi'ah* are in the whole country of Pakistan, for example? Besides, these large collections are for the specialist, not for people like us. Reading them we would become confused. In them there are things that are not totally applicable nor necessarily authentic. At the moment there is no collection that is both reliable and of a reasonable length, about a thousand pages. This resource will soon be made available, but it is long overdue.

As well as having access to a textbook explaining the Qur'an and a collection of hadiths that is usable,. we need a book of *shari'ah*, a textbook on Islamic law. It is obligatory for every Muslim to adhere to the *shari'ah;* he therefore needs a book which he will use day in, day out. Amongst the Shi'ah the book that they will consult will be a treatise by a living jurist. Yet I assure you that these treatises are 99.9% the same because they are based on a common body of hadiths. If we look at the treatises which the jurists have written over the last six hundred years, we will find that there is no change even in the sequence of the points of law. Therefore, what is needed is a treatise of not more than two hundred pages, with the footnotes of a traditional jurist. In this way, even if we do not follow that particular jurist, we will have the points of law which do not change. And the points which do change will be no more than thirty or forty at most. For example, many of the schools of law differ concerning the determination of the distance of travel at which the prayer must be shortened. The point of difference lies in where one begins to count the number of miles of travel. Is it from one's house? Or is it from the boundary of one's town or district? The legal decrees of the jurists differ on this matter according to the school of law which they accept. What I wish to emphasize is that in trying to reactivate and revitalize our religion we need aids. To achieve our goal, there are three requirements: a) need; b) those who can fulfil the need — the scholars; and c) the means of fulfilling the need. What we are discussing now is the means. Essentially it is a kit comprising of:

1.   A good Qur'an with a good, simple commentary in it, acceptable, modern, contemporary and usable.

2.   A good collection of enough hadiths.

We are living at a time in which we all share the need for these resource materials. They will be made available if we genuinely want to use them. Why is it that they are not already available? Allah is not unjust. He says in the Qura'an:

> We did not wrong them but they wronged them-
> selves.
>
> (2:57)

We need to revive our religion and to live by our Qur'an and by our glorious beloved Prophet, yet we are unable to do so because the means are not available, in the form of human beings as well as in the form of books, publications, and so on. This only means that the demand is not real. We must first recognize the malaise and the need for a cure, then the means to overcome the illness will manifest. Then we can all live Islam without segregating Islamic studies from worldly studies. In recent times there has been much discussion about Islamic economics, yet Islamic banking, the basis for this economics, is something which does not exist. Islamic banking is a lie because the foundation for it is non-existent. As far as 'good loan' is concerned, it is done without imposing a condition. If you do, it is usury *(riba)*. If we offer a loan, it is appropriate to receive our money back without an increase. But nowadays, as we all know, every country in the world is experiencing inflation. As a result, there is no permissible loan policy and nobody is telling us what to do, nobody dares.

The greatest scholar amongst us would not dare to say that many of the activities of Muharram are obnoxious, let alone forbidden *(haram)*, though he may say so privately. Therefore, between the *'ulama* class and the masses, concerning certain aspects of Islam, there is a wide gap. This is mentioned not to criticize the *'ulama*, on the contrary, it is mentioned to point out that if the truth were pointed out by them, they would probably lose all connection with the people. It is better to have something rather than nothing. At least during the ten days of Muharram they remember Imam Husayn — it doesn't matter in what fashion. If this practice were exposed and stopped, then the people would have nothing.

But we want to go beyond whatever inheritance we have, whatever superstition we have, beyond what might be called the veneer, in order to attain the inner meaning. And that cannot occur unless we demand to know — this is both our right and our duty. *Ijtihad*, striving, is a necessary condition upon everyone, but according to the *shari'ah*, only a few members of a community must specialize in the Islamic sciences, whereas everyone of us must strive to attain knowledge of the *shari'ah*, and the more we apply our knowledge, the more we find the boundaries of the *shari'ah* are for our own protection. Most young Muslims nowadays refuse to accept the *shari'ah* because they have not tasted the benefit of its boundaries.

For example, we are enjoined to lower our gaze. I shall never forget the very fine Iranian man from New York who came to our conference in San Antonio where we were living away from city life. He came directly from New York where every part of a woman is exposed. After a period of time spent in our protected environment, he came to realize how much of his energy had been dissipated by sexual excitement from the advertising media, from the barbaric Western so-called culture.

Unless we believe in Islam by finding, through practice, that its bounds are of direct benefit to us, we will never adhere to it. We have come to understand that it is for our benefit to lower our eyes so that we do not become excited. For if we become excited, we will have a desire, and if we have a desire, we will have to satisfy it, because our minds will have become engaged

with it. Lowering the eyes is for our benefit. The veil *(hijab)* is
not to punish the woman. Actually, it is for her protection. A
woman's role within nature is to attract a man and thereby
unfold the plot that each one of us is hatching. But Allah is the
ultimate plotter. He says:

> You plot and I plot and I am the best of plotters.
>   (8:30)

If we really do want to renew our lives, then that desire will
produce the means. It is a question of a balance of economics —
supply and demand. If we want to have the Qur'an, we must
be free to challenge it. We find that one part of it will prove its
other part and thereby give us a complete picture. For he who
dives into the Qur'an, the allegorical *ayats* will become firm, clear
ayats, along with the rest of the Qur'an. How can it be otherwise,
since the author is He Who is the Most Decisive. "Take what
comes to you easily from it" and move on; one should not be
scholastic, academic and rhetorical as is taught in the so-called
'western education'. One should not debate or argue about the
basic principles of Islam. Things are either clear or unclear. The
artist knows that the grey that he sees is composed of black and
white. For the discriminating being, it is similar. Every one of
us has been given the capacity to discriminate clearly between
right and wrong. If this were not true where would Allah's justice
be? The Prophet, may the peace and blessings of Allah be upon
him and his family, said: "In your life you will recognize things
that are correct and clear — Do them! You will also discover
things you know are not correct — do not do them! And in between there are areas which are doubtful — avoid them!"

The Prophet has pointed to the fact that we know intuitively
what is right and wrong. With this knowledge we can learn the
correct courtesy towards the creation and towards the Qur'an.

It is up to us to take from the Qur'an what we can digest;
and then take more and more so we may gain in strength. Instead
of that we become academic, thinking of abstruse questions. In
my case I was rude to one of my masters, asking the question:
"How should I fast if I am living at the north pole, because there

the sun never sets completely?" He replied, "You idiot! Send me a postcard when you are there and I'll tell you!" The question had no relevance to my life. I was not going to go to the north pole. The Prophet, may the peace and blessings of Allah be upon him and his family, said: "Give me knowledge that is useful." There is no benefit in seeking information that does not provide us with the correct courtesy towards Allah, the creation and ourselves. What have we become but a people who neither enjoy this world nor the next. At least the unbeliever has a fling here. Imam 'Ali Zayn al-'Abidin, upon him be peace, said, "For the believer this world is like a filthy, dusty, stinking gown; when he removes it, his soul is free." In fact, he has already tasted freedom, otherwise, he could not have possessed certain know-ledge, *yaqin*. Also, the Imam said, "As far as the believer is concerned, this world is his wedding gown." At least he has his wedding gown here. We have neither what this world nor what the next world has to offer — as is demonstrated by our life-style, which is part eastern and part imitation western. I do not mean to say that we should not live comfortably, joyfully and with great integrity, but we have become a nation of third-grade imitators.

In the last fifty years a technological gap has widened between East and West. The Muslims have been unable to absorb their own culture. Although they have their own pure cotton and wool, they import vast amounts of synthetic materials which electrocute them when they wear them. In the East, discriminating people are realizing the importance of pure materials. We have lost what we had. The Muslims living in the West are truly the worst off. They have lost what they had. Their younger generation is calling them to question. In England there are about 1.5 million Muslims out of a total population of 54 or 55 million. There is not one member of parliament amongst them. The Jews on the other hand, number just over 300,000 in England. They have thirty-eight or thirty-nine members of parliament. It is a reflec-tion of our own reality: no two Muslim households are united; every mosque is fighting with its neighbouring mosque. Can you imagine? There is no reality in the Islam that is being practised in England.

Thirty years ago in Karbala when I left, there was not a single hotel or restaurant. It was, in fact, considered shameful to take someone to a restaurant. Although I have not been to Karbala for twenty years, I would not be surprised if it were actually fashionable to entertain a guest at a restaurant. There is nothing left of either Karbala or Najaf. In the name of modernity, every fabric of life has been torn apart. In striving to have a beautiful home, the people have moved away from the bazaar. Now to get to the bazaar a car is necessary, and of course to have a car, money is necessary. The average man has become a slave of the bank manager. And the result has been the destruction of the Islamic society.

We cannot go back to what Karbala was. It is not possible. But we do have to consider the set of values which we are passing on to the young. Because of the younger people's demands, the challenges facing us and the realization that western society is on the verge of collapse, we are, thank God, beginning to awaken.

I have just come from India. There, I met young people, businessmen, dynamic people who are successful, all of whom were saying: "Look, we want to contain ourselves. We know that material success is not incompatible with spiritual success, but we are thirsty for knowledge." But as I have already said there is no material to help them to know. There is not a single Qur'an which is useful to them, nor a collection of hadiths, nor a good history or biography of the Prophet Muhammad.

Many people whom I see, and to whom I am attracted are discriminating and intelligent people who realize that after this life there is death. They want to know what this life means. Is it fair that after years of gathering knowledge, experience and wisdom, we are recycled back to the worms? What is the purpose of this life? What is behind the things we see? What is this invisible hand that manifests in the visible? How does the inter-link occur between them? Where can we find the code of conduct to follow that will bring us to safety? How can we live joyfully at all times, irrespective of the outer situation? How can we be in a situation where we are able to perceive cause and effect and yet retain our trust and faith that there is something beyond cause and effect?

Our lives are composed of a mechanistic side and a spiritual side. There is scientific, informational knowledge and there is spiritual knowledge. And Allah says in a *Hadith Qudsi:* "I was a hidden treasure and I wanted to be known, so I created (the world) to be known." Allah's purpose in creation is to unveil His knowledge to those who have purified and unveiled their hearts. These are the ones who have given in charity and have moved on the straight path, the *sirat al-mustaqim,* and then have found that there is no path. When they go through the door of 'Ali, they find that there is no door. They were already there in the companionship of those who have awakened in this life before their awakening in the next. The Prophet, may the peace and blessings of Allah be upon him and his family, says: "Die before you die." He is not talking about the death of our bodies, but of the death of our whims, desires, lusts, expectations, fears and anxieties. If we kill them, we will find that we are alive with pure life and consciousness. Otherwise, we are as Imam 'Ali says: "As walking tombs." But also the Prophet said: "If you want to look at a dead person walking, look at me!" Does it mean that he was a dead being? Would so many thousands have fallen in love with and done anything for a dead being? What he meant was that he was dead to all the things which they, who possessed childish consciousness, were killing each other for. Die to those things and rise above them and you will find that it is all very easy. The Prophet said: "To remember Allah for one hour is better than to spend seventy years of worship in prayers." Worship without knowledge is actually not worship at all. He also said, "The sleep of a scholar who knows is better than a whole night of worship of he who has no knowledge."

So the purpose of our gathering is to obtain knowledge, the knowledge that is rooted within us. But because we have allowed ourselves to become overgrown with the concerns of this life, this knowledge has had no chance to grow. So we have to pluck out the weeds of concern. As the people of gnosis say: "First we must empty ourselves." And how do we do this except by recognizing that cheating one another is of no use and that hoarding is of no use. By experience we learn that these things are not going to make us happier. The reason why we want money is to have the potential of freeing ourselves from future desires. So then why have future desires? It is so simple. Once we learn this then emptying out becomes sweet. Once our fear of death and concerns for provision in this life are weeded out, the process of displacing our old values by higher timeless values becomes a joy. Old people in the West desire to live on in this life out of the fear of death. Because of the way they have lived their lives, they have no access to the discovery of the immortality within themselves. They are barred from the light of the Prophet, the Messenger of Allah.

It is very difficult to bring the message of Islam to the people of the West. They have been taught to be free like children. They have outward freedom and inward constrictions, the reverse of our way which is outward constriction, courtesy, and inward freedom, illumination. Therefore, they do not want Muhammad the Messenger of Allah. They can accept the concept of Reality and unification but they cannot accept the principle of Prophethood because they have been spoiled. Imam 'Ali said: "If you sit where you want as a child, you will not be sitting where you want as an adult." As children they were not groomed, and therefore the fruit which they bear is bitter. And as a result women are without guidance because there are no men. The world is run by women because we have failed to fulfil our reality as men (Contrary to the contemporary social situation, a woman wants to be contained. She wants the attention that a pearl receives when it is put in a fine protective box with love and care. She wants to be protected not as a prisoner but as something cherished.)

We, in our superficial understanding of Islam, abuse our women and refuse to permit them their own lives. Our values are upside down. In the so-called 'Islamic World' a man's hand is cut off if he steals two rupees, but if he steals billions he is made a national hero. Such injustice is rampant because we are only applying the parts of the *shari'ah* which suit us. It will not work! Allah says that He will bring people whom He loves and who love Him to replace the people who have proven unfaithful to Him. Allah says in the Qur'an:

> And you will not find any change in Allah's way.

The Prophet was not outside the arena of trial. During the Battle of Uhud an arrow flew towards his mouth, striking his teeth and breaking them. But the Prophet's heart was with Allah and all he could say was: "Oh Allah! Forgive my companions for abandoning me, they are ignorant. I remain with them because I am your servant and slave in order to illumine their hearts." He did not complain.

So we see by the Prophet's example that the believer is at all times inwardly content and contained, and outwardly struggling and doing his best. When called upon, he serves, and when left to himself, he recognizes that he is in the hand of his Creator. He is joyful, seeing nothing other than His mercy.

It is up to us. I beseech you to call upon Allah and demand this certainty. We all have the same fears, anxieties, doubts and suspicions. If we truly want to awaken, it will happen: the means will become available; the men will step forward from amongst us. It is no use imagining that someone will come from elsewhere to help. The help will come from amongst us. This is the way of Allah. For those of us who have been awakened, there is no such thing as a miracle, rather everything is a miracle: our existence, our breath, every moment transforms us. There are laws and there are exceptions, always. There cannot be a rule without its exception. And why should we look for an exception to a rule which we have not yet grasped?

I pray to Allah to enable us to rise with our glorious heritage which is Islam in its true meaning and essence, based on faith. I beseech you to demand it and look for it. You will find that it is already there. But it needs to be activated by being made part of our lives. The knowledge of Islam which remains is purely academic and informational and has no transformative character; it is barren. We want to transform ourselves. We want to become joyful, correct and fearless, fearing only transgression of the laws of nature and reality. We want to be obedient to One God, One Reality; and to be a slave to One Reality, not a slave to other creations. We are, essentially, the inheritors of Allah's deputy, the Prophet Adam. But we have to rise to it, demand it and be it. By evolving our Islam together, joyfully, correctly, and cheerfully, a new society will emerge and the whole world will change its mind about Islam. Presently, it is a name without a reality because we have not made it real in our hearts.

6

Good News

There is no good news *(bisharah)* without a warning *(nidharah)*.
After all the universe hangs on opposites. I would like to warn
you of what is happening thoughout the world. We cannot sit
at ease in this time and expect to be able to practise the true
path of Islam, both outwardly and inwardly, without being attacked in one way or another. Until recently there were many
citadels of Islam that could not be penetrated. These no longer
exist. We have inadvertently become exposed. If we do not recognize it fully, we have not recognized the symptoms of a sick
patient, and we are all patients in this world. We have come as
sick people in order to wake up, to prepare ourselves to meet
our Creator. From where illness comes there also comes the cure.

As we have discovered, the situation we are in is extremely
sensitive and precarious. There are more and more institutions
devoted to technological know-how. The word *shahadah* used to
be used in relation to martyrdom. Now if you ask an Arab what
it means, he will tell you a B.A. or B.Sc. from some western
university.

It is not that we should be against science, against causality,
but we must put it in its proper place. This is not the purpose
of our creation. Science is a tool to help provide basic existential
harmony in order that we may get on with the real business,
which is knowledge of Allah. There is no other business. All
other business is useless, senseless and secondary, and will cause
our doom if it does not support the business of obtaining knowledge of Allah. But our so-called technological education has
taken over. Our young people have become spoiled and ruined
through useless academic pursuits.

We are following the same path taken by Christianity. The
Christian Church was robbed of its essential teaching and offered
only a set of dogmas and a lot of useless doctrine. The intelligent
people refrained from attacking it because they knew that man's
nature tends toward dogmatism. Therefore, they circumvented
the Church by hiding under the guise of scientific endeavour
and logic. Over a period of time the churches crumbled. Now

they are being sold as bingo halls. Everywhere in the world, from Spain to South America, there are churches up for sale — they do not know what to do with them. Science has prevailed. The Church has now become subservient to science. All of the endeavours that were sponsored by the Church 150 years ago are now under secular control. This so-called Godless scientific endeavour has taken over because there was nothing better. There was no unitary knowledge, no full, integrated message. There was no Qur'an and there was no prophetic practice.

Now there is outer technology and no inner technology, no spiritual doctrine. We in the East are importing and developing the outer technology without having it balanced with the inner technology that supersedes it. We do not realize the importance of making our outer progress subservient to our inner progress. The promise of Allah, however, is that His way will prevail whether we like it or not. But, if we are sensible and intelligent, we had better like it, and we had better learn to become the hand of Allah, His instrument. Otherwise, He will eventually find other people to fulfil His designs. The Light of Allah will prevail as Allah has said in the Qur'an. Eventually, a time will come when the earth will be inherited by those who are close to Allah.

If we truly wish to become the instruments of Allah, we must work to arrest the anomalous situation which I have just described and to do this, we will have to readjust our priorities. Knowledge of the material world is not the first priority. As we have stated previously, materialistic knowledge is magnificient if it is used for Allah's sake — for enhancing our knowledge of Allah. As Imam 'Ali said: "Doing without, the life of abstention, does not mean that one does not own or control anything. Rather it means that one is not owned or controlled by anything." We are not against matter. Matter is the creation of Allah. We are against accumulation of it and attachment to it.

We are no fools. People have been abused and thought not to be intelligent. The mass media which have been the cause of a great deal of our decadence and corruption will also reveal to us the truth. A source of evil may also be a source of goodness. What I want to point out to you and share with you is the danger. In the past we had more discrimination and what was not correct was fairly obvious. We could catch it by easily discerning its characteristics and reject it as unacceptable. That is no longer possible, for what is incorrect has become interwoven with what is correct in so many different formats. We have become accustomed to this arrangement of things and we think we are protected. But we are not. In fact it is harmful to us in every way. Our habits, our manners, our way of life, our economies, our banking system, our monetary system have all become diluted, and in many cases taken over, by the system of materialism which is continually spurred on by greed. Our ability to distinguish has become very weak. The people who have intentionally sold themselves to this system have no respect for anything except their own selfish, inner and lower animalistic desires. If we do not sharpen our inner wits and develop our inner technology, the knowledge of the self, we will be swallowed up by this system.

We must begin to state formally and make common knowledge the true nature of 'modernism' for this expose will protect those who can listen and act upon what they have heard. It does not matter if we are accused of being backward or dogmatic. Modernism is not sacrosanct. We are all for progress — the progress of man towards his Creator.

> O man! surely you must strive (to attain) to your
> Lord, a hard striving until you meet Him.
>
> (84:6)

This is progress. In fact we can have that encounter here and now instantly — if we are willing to let go and drop everything. Then we can see nothing other than the hand of Allah.

We are for progress, but what they call progress is often regress. We often allow ourselves to be swept away by slogans like democracy. We live in a dangerous time and no clear revitalization of the necessary is plainly evident, except possibly in Iran, where thousands have been hit by the light of Allah and are sustained in a glorious state of abandonment by continually facing death in the way of Allah. A great deal of Islamic sentiment has been kindled by the Iranian revolution in the last seven or eight years. It has become a vogue now because many heads of state are disturbed by it but cannot stop it. If they resist it, it will grow, and if they give lip service to it, it will also grow. This is the way of Allah. It will grow no matter what they do, it is Allah's business. But what are we going to do about it?

We have a great responsibility now, more than at any other time. There are no longer those natural barriers that we could have used in the past. All that is left for us is to develop stronger and stronger inner awareness, coupled with outer practices, so that everyone of us is a citadel, so that every household itself is an enclosed city, waiting for the blessed Prophet, to be their guest. If we fail to be a living reality and manifestation of Islam, then we have closed the door and all we can do is espouse false hope.

Events do not happen in a superstitious way. If we are with Allah, then we understand Allah's way. If we are very far removed, then we see only other than Allah's way. What we have said is true regarding the causality of physical experience, yet the man of Allah sees nothing other than miracles. Everything he sees is a miracle, because he knows that Allah is behind it all, using causality to manifest events. The man of Allah is totally abandoned to the experience of being in Allah's hands with his faculty of intelligence and reason fully awakened. We are people of unity. This is the path of unity, the unification of the outer and the inner, practice and belief, intention and action. We do not separate the intention from the action. We do not separate belief from good action.

The times we are living in are very difficult and very delicate. The enemy is subtle. Our revival and awakening must be in a manner that contemporary man can understand. Dusting off our predecessors is not sufficient. Allah says in the Qur'an:

> Whatever communications We abrogate or cause
> to be forgotten, We bring one better than it or like
> it.
>
> (2:106)

In other words, Allah will not withdraw a 'sign' without replacing it by one that is better. That means that men of knowledge now are better than the men of knowledge before in that they are appropriate for their age.

If we cannot present the truth in the present day, in the present language which is acceptable to the young, we will have lost them to outer technological qualifications that will only enhance their materialistic situation and further their loss. Everybody will have an isolated house and one or two cars. How incredibly boring. How can Islam live in that fashion? Islam is about gatheredness. Our style of life reflects the fact that we have become diluted and that our Islam is by inheritance not by action. Muslims by birth are afraid that they will be labelled as backward or religious. This is because their knowledge of Islam has not become connected to the time in which they live. The Muslims have become soft and indiscriminate.

> O you who believe! Do not take the Jews and the Christians for friends (allies); whoever amongst you takes them for a friend, then surely he is one of them; surely Allah does not guide the unjust people.
>
> (5:51)

This is our situation. If we do not recognize it and act upon what we recognize, we will be swamped. To reiterate the remedy, inner technology must prevail over outer technology and it has to be done by inner technologists who will come to the market place. This is not the day of sitting behind walls in isolation. This is the day for translating the little knowledge we have into action. If we do that, we will succeed.

We visited Malaysia where we attended the Friday prayer in the main mosque in Kuala Lumpur. It was the most boring, sleep-making discourse. Allah would have blessed us more if we had gone to sleep in that discourse than to have listened to that fellow. Wine and drinks flow everywhere in Malaysia. There was a puddle of wine in every single place we stepped in, and yet the man recited the verses of the Qur'an regarding the consumption of alcohol and gambling as though they had nothing to do with what was going on around him. People came into the mosque like sheep, fulfilling their Islamic obligation. We sat there like idiots and did not know what to do. The mosque was full and they were bragging that it can house thirty to forty thousand people — thirty to forty thousand incompetent, so-called 'Muslims'. Not one of them got up and shouted or screamed to say, 'Why the hell is he not talking about how to stop the alcohol and gambling that has saturated our country?' The King was sitting there and consumption of alcohol and gambling occurred everywhere in that country. We tried to find a so-called Muslim rest-house to stay in and finally found one. We also found the bottles of liquor kept for guests who so desired. The non-Muslim hostels are better because at least they are honest. Hypocrisy occurs in degrees, it is not black or white. So many things were revealed to the Prophet about the hypocrites around him that it was thought no one would be spared.

The Prophet was a superman in his inwardness, not in his outwardness. Outwardly he suffered. Inwardly, he did not mind what happened, because he knew it was the will of Allah and he saw the laws of Allah perfectly manifested. If we want to live as truly worthy followers of that greatest of all beings, then we have to really fully understand and live Islam. Otherwise we merely congratulate each other, exchanging *'Id* cards. The true way of Islam expounded in the Qur'an, which encompasses us and is within us, combined with the way of Muhammad, is the only way in this world and the Hereafter. If we are not totally immersed, we will remain petty creatures, or people who give Islamic study certificates. When and by whom were these formal schools and Islamic study departments created? It is because there are not enough of us truly in Islam that we have to create these specialized institutions.

Incumbent upon every Muslim is the knowledge of how to live and practise Islam. But since we have abandoned this knowledge we have created specialists instead. The point here is that we may end up having a priestly class while the rest of us will only attend some ritual for occasional, superstitious, sentimental or ceremonial purposes.

We may be exaggerating the situation a little, but this is necessary in order to highlight the dangers. The criticism applies to all of us. We must aim to bring forth young people who can take the real message of Islam to the world including the West. These poor wretched people have had a raw deal. The Americans, for instance, have not received the message. They have been made into mechanical robots slaving away for their bank manager. We must have sympathy, but there is also a limit to what can be done for them. Many of them have gone too far. We cannot sow seeds on rock and expect them to germinate.

In order to bring Islam to others we must bring it forth in ourselves. If not, then it is very difficult to convince anybody. If our hearts are won by technological glitter and have not been exposed to inner awakening and inner delights, then we will end up being the decadent and corrupt, because that is the story of man. Our hearts must be filled with something, if not with inner delights, submission, worship, and the love of reality, they will be filled inadvertently by outer distractions which will cause our eventual destruction.

We must move positively now and delete incorrect attitudes and actions, cut out what is corrupting us, not saying through false hope that we will be safe or Allah will save us all on account of our good acts. Vinegar will ruin the honey unless it is kept in another pot. This is the way of Allah. We must have discrimination and act. We must strive for that inner awakening that will bring about the knowledge of unity, so that Islam will prevail in every way of life, be it economic, political or spiritual, both inside the mosque and outside.

7

Accountability

Everyone is accountable.

> Nay! Man is evidence against himself,
> Though he puts forth his excuses.
>
> (75:14–15)

We may give excuses, but we want to know Allah and it is Allah's promise that we will come to know Him. We will see nothing other than Allah, and this is the inner meaning of "There is no god but Allah."

The believer is always inwardly content with the Decree of Allah. Outwardly he is enslaved, doing his utmost with as pure an intention as he can possibly muster. A prophetic *hadith* relates that, "All actions are according to the intentions behind them and every individual receives what he intended." The message of Islam is simple, clear and direct.

Islam was spread by those who lived it, whose lives and actions reflected it; not by preaching, threatening or haranguing, nor by destruction. It was propagated by people who behaved totally in unison with their Creator's laws. Following in the footsteps of the Prophet, they were correct first with themselves, then with their families, then with their neighbours. A prophetic *hadith* relates that the near ones are more deserving of one's love. First, one has mercy upon oneself. By doing so, one will see the Beneficent and will recognize His mercy. Then, one moves on to those closest: one's family, those for whom one is responsible; then, one's neighbours; then, one's society at large, and finally the entirety of mankind. This is how the process of Islam begins and increases. The centre from which that beginning occurs is oneself. We cannot simply hope, superstitiously, that someone will arise to bring about an inner revolution of the heart, to create a heart that is not attached.

It is only through this inner revolution that all of us can evolve to become healthy, filled with love not pride. Outwardly a Muslim may be humble, but he is not oppressed because his humility is the product of knowledge. Outward oppression is not acceptable to a Muslim. Either Muslims rule, or else they are in enemy territory waiting for the day when they will rule. There is no compromise, for systems other than Islam do not provide justice. If Islam rules, then all who are under its umbrella and accept its rules are protected according to the injunctions of its Divine Law.

> Surely they think it [this reckoning] is far off.
> And We see it nigh.
>
> (70:6–7)

The people of Allah see everything clearly. He who acts unjustly will be recompensed accordingly, sometimes in this life, sometimes in the next. One is lucky if the recompense is in this life. The true believer will always receive his account immediately. He cannot get away with anything. This is a sign of Allah's love for him. The Qur'an tells us not to look at those who seem to get away with their transgressions. They may look well and wealthy, but we do not know what is hidden inside. Often we see homes that are palaces on the outside but tombs on the inside. Recently, while on a trip to Malaysia, we came upon a hut belonging to a poor man, a lover of Allah. It was a tiny hut, a shanty with no roof, but the man inside was a light of Allah. Immediately afterwards, we went to someone's palace where we had been invited. The limousines and sports cars were lined up at the entrance, but inside it was like a tomb . It was only by Allah's mercy that we managed to escape quickly. If the inner is not there, the outer is of no use. If the inner is there, the outer does not matter. We will get what we deserve, not what we desire. It is a scientific formula, perfect. It is Allah's balance. This world is cosmic, not chaotic. It does not depend upon our wishes. Did not the blessed Prophet wish the best for his people? Allah says in the Glorious Qur'an:

> Surely you cannot guide whom you love, but Allah
> guides whom He pleases, and He knows best the
> followers of the right way.
>
> (28:56)

So many of us have close relatives who are at a great loss. It is our duty to do our best to be available at all times to help them, but other than that there is nothing we can do. If we learn to allow our heart to turn freely, then we will discover the truth behind our existence, and everyone else's existence. We will find the true meaning of:

> And We created you from one self.
>
> (4:1)

All of us are the same, experiencing love, hate, insecurity, companionship, brotherhood, enmity. We are conscious of all these things, even sleep. What an incredible thing it is that we should say, 'I slept well.' What does this mean? What an incredible statement! 'I' — who is this I? If we have not evolved spiritually, then that 'I' is Shaytan (Satan). It says in the Qur'an:

> He (Shaytan) said: I am better than he; You have created me from fire, while him You created of dust.
>
> (7:12)

This is the rise of the ego. 'I am better than you because I accomplished this.' The rise of the ego hides Allah, and the ego will remain until one recognizes its presence at all times. That recognition itself will put the Shaytan on a tether. But Shaytan is a great teacher because through him we suffer, causing us to grow into what is our actual potential. Look at the diamond. It is an ordinary pebble. The greatest suffering it can endure is to be cut by an expert hand. Yet that cutting brings out its potential as an incredible reflector of light. In reality it is just a stone made of carbon, but people will kill each other for it and turn countries upside down in order to obtain it.

Islam has always been the path, and there have always been great Muslims everywhere, where you least expect them. If the path of Islam is not practised at every moment, opportunities are being missed. How long are we going to live? It is the remembrance of death which causes us to take advantage of the opportunities in this life. Death does not make us morbid or depressed, on the contrary it spurs us on at every moment. Life is our only capital. Every investment, every asset is replaceable except life. It is counted with every breath, and that count is registered subchromosomically in our cells. Every cell tells the entire story. This is the meaning of the Qur'anic verse,

> On that Day We will set a seal upon their mouths,
> and their hands shall speak to Us, and their feet
> shall bear witness of what they earned.
>
> (36:65)

Every soul contains within it the entire genetic story and its unfoldment. Time is short but the opportunities are plentiful, so we must start from where we arc. This is what is real, there is no supersitition in it.

The Qur'an is the foundation of the path of Islam and one must immediately begin to work with it. It must not be left to the experts who study it for themselves. Everyone who has written an explanation of the Qur'an has tried to fathom it for himself. Now we must do the same, not accepting blindly what others say. We must interpret it correctly and be convinced of what it says. If we are not convinced, then we are not connected to the source from which the Qur'an came, we are not in unity. At first, we accept what it says until a time will come when we know with certainty. If we take the Qur'an fully, we will recognize that it is unfolding within us, and that is the meaning of *taqwa* (fearful awareness). *Taqwa* is to avoid something that is not propitious. It is to take preventive action. This word does not translate readily into English. It is like fear, but it is the fear which wells up in one through the knowledge that when one transgresses into the unknown there will be trouble. It is like being on a highway — If I deviate from the road, I have *taqwa* of the verge because if I hit it, I will suffer. It is we who will suffer from the consequences of transgression. *Taqwa* is not a fear caused by the opporession of a tyrant who may punish us. It is peculiar to *taqwa* and many other Arabic words that when they are translated into English, or any Latin-based Roman language, they usually become biblical, Christian and misleading in meaning.

Do not be intimidated by the Arabic of the Qur'an. Take whatever can help you and move on. Ask Allah for His mercy. The knowledge is already within us, but ignorance has covered it. Our situation is like that of a person who has to dig a well. Someone's help may be necessary to point out the right location. When moisture appears, one feels encouraged and eventually the spring issues forth. Do not be afraid. It is there, it is ours, so we must claim it from the One and Only Source from which we have all come. We are sustained by the mercy of that Source, and we will return to it in great comfort and peace at the moment of the experience called death. The word for death in Arabic comes from the same verbal root that yields a word which means loyalty, honesty. The created being is loyal to its origin. His soul returns to his Lord and his body to dust.

In many parts of the world, people are beginning to find that materialism is not producing the happiness that man thought it would. It is correct for us to have the basic tranquillity attained when there is enough food to stop the stomach from aching and when the body is protected from heat and cold. But having achieved this, we get carried away by the idea that we need more and more. We become insecure. For instance, today, in many of the so-called oil rich-countries, it is more important than anything else to have a private plane. There are hundreds of them registered in Jeddah alone. One man may have three, two of them being Boeing 707s. The staff for his planes cost him something like 1.8 million dollars a year. And he only travels four or five times a year.

> And the life of this world is nothing but a provision
> of vanities.
>
> (3:185)

One may spend an increasing amount of time accumulating wealth which will lead, necessarily, to a decrease in time spent in other areas of one's life. One may begin to spend so little time with one's family that, having brought up one's child, one may end up complaining, 'but I sent him to the best schools and gave him every opportunity. Look at the rascal, he is wholly ungrateful.' This poor fellow does not realize that his child wanted love, his time and attention. He did not want to be sent to a boarding school. He wanted to be part of a family.

> O You men! Surely We have created you of a male
> and a female, and made you tribes and families
> that you may know each other.
>
> (49:13)

Man is a social being, but once every house becomes a villa, people lose touch with their neighbours. We are not denying comfort, or basic living, but the style must be conducive to a vital, correct way.

We must continuously thank Allah for this great gift of life, for the responsibility that He has given to man who is His representative on this earth. We must continuously thank Allah for the path of knowledge He has given man through the awakening of his intellect so that, in this short experience, he may behave in a godly manner. We must continuously thank Allah for the blessedness of the provisions he has given us on this short journey so that we may become confirmed in our certainty and place our trust only in Him. We must continuously thank Allah for the opportunity to serve, because if we do not serve in the way of Allah, we will be serving other than in the way of Allah, for there is no stationariness in this existence. If we do not move upward, then we move downward. We have all come to this existence to experience the Creator's laws and to discriminate and decide, through experience, what to do and what not to do, in order to act safely, correctly, courageously and nobly in this short life in preparation for the timeless zone in the next. We are bound by that absolute Decree. There is no discussion. Either one is in submission or not, and if one is truly in Islam, then one will know the taste and the meaning of trust and faith. The rest is a lot of discussion, books and Islamic studies departments. If our knowledge does not become internalized and lived totally, we have missed the point. Islam is the perfect way to be, and to be implies that you are free and pure from yesterday, because you have done your best. It also implies that you have no fears, desires or expectations for tomorrow, for the true man of submission is and tastes beingness.

Those of us who have inherited our Islam, this great gift, do
not realize its real value. We take it for granted, like a child who
does not know the value of a gem. We are fortunate to have been
brought up in an atmosphere where the name of Allah is recited
and where the hearts of so many people throb with love for His
Prophet.

Life has not been bargained for by us. We have not bought it
in a market place. We have obtained it from our Creator and
He may take it away at any time. Thus it is a great honour to
be given this opportunity to be able to share in it. We are here
together in this existence in order to remind each other of the
meaning of our existence, of the true inner and outer meaning
of Islam, the glory, majesty and beauty that results from true
abandonment with the awakening of the intellect. We are not
here to remind each other by abandoning ourselves to ignorance,
superstition, sentimentality and hypocrisy.

So often we see examples of people who have come to Islam
through an existential bargain. They are good to God and God
is good to them. However, Allah is good to all.

And My mercy encompasses all things.

(7:156)

His mercy encompasses everything, whether we recognize it or
not. It is up to us to recognize Allah's mercy, even in circumstances that are very inconvenient, even in situations where
we may find a great deal of injustice. That injustice is also a
part of Allah's Decree. Allah has given man the license to live
justly according to His laws, or unjustly according to His laws.
We have that option. Allah also tells us that eventually He will
triumph. Eventually His light, meaning the knowledge of Truth,
will encompass everything. Our existence is secondary. If our
fundamental objective is not the One and Only Source of existence, then we will merely receive diluted versions of the message.
These diluted versions, which we have witnessed throughout the
few years of our life, can cause nothing other than dispersion,
disagreement, argument, opinions and debate. If our objective
is not to see unity in diversity, then we have missed the point.

Knowledge of this world, so-called scientific knowledge, is

based on the understanding of causality. In fact, all materialistic advancement is based on causality. It is very simple and mechanistic. It is outward technology — purchaseable. One spends time and energy, but whatever one learns has no meaning unless it is made subservient to the all-encompassing knowledge of the Source of existence — the Creator Whose way is manifest and non-manifest, visible and invisible; Whose creation is like a dot manifested on the vast unseen which is an environment of powers, forces and waves that are beyond physical perception. Any intelligent person who accepts the physical world will also accept the unseen. This physical world is but a gross manifestation of something that is subtle. A human being develops naturally through life from the subtle to the gross and then back to the subtle again.

A child is born programmed in submission, all ready to discover reality. That is the meaning of the Prophetic narration that every child is born a Muslim. Every child is born in submission to Allah, not knowing to what world he is coming to. Think of the environment of the womb. It is aquatic and well insulated, in such a way that the child hears nothing other than the heart of the mother which sounds like Allah, Allah, Allah. For nine months, this is what the child in the womb hears. Then, within a split second, it is cut off from that warm and protected environment and exposed to the air. It is a tremendous shock. All of us come into this world in shock and leave it in shock, except for those who long for the experience of death, and who do not look upon it in the normal way. This is the reason why the true believers give up their lives with a smile. They know there is something far greater ahead.

"What is the condition of my slaves?" asks Allah in the sacred narration, "They seek ease in this life and I did not create it for ease." Allah created life in order to see whether we are wise enough to recognize what is behind it all; whether we are intelligent enough to discover that we can never control this world, no matter who we are, even if we are the most powerful kings or dictators. We have come to go. The worms are already waiting in the grave to nibble at us. This may be very inconvenient for us, yet it is the absolute reality of our condition. The knowledge and full acceptance of death leads to abandonment and freedom in life. It is all there for one to see and to glorify, so we may have a most wonderful time, expecting to have a better time in the next experience. One knows, however, that this can never last, one can never be in control. As soon as we have good health, wealth is lost. As soon as we acquire wealth, health deteriorates. As soon as one acquires good companionship, one's wife falls ill or one's parents die. It is Allah's mercy upon us to remind us of the reality and objective of our existence.

One of the general faults or weaknesses to which a born Muslim is prone, is to think that Islam is for somebody else. He thinks that the Qur'an, the teaching and the way of the Prophet are for someone else because he imagines that these are things which he already possesses. But familiarity breeds contempt. The responsibility is actually greater for a born Muslim, for he has had more opportunity: the advantage of growing up in an environment where Allah was glorified, with warmth and affection, can also be a great disadvantage if one has not internalized and lived it.

So we are born in ignorance in order for us to increase in knowledge as we grow up into adults. We are programmed. Our agitations, insecurities, anxieties, loves and hates are all programmed by the One and only Creator who encompasses all, in order for us to move on from the world of gross physicality to the world of subtle meaning — from the outer existential situation to inner abandonment, submission and contentment. Outwardly, we can never be content. Even if the whole world becomes our slave, we know that we will soon die. How can we be content? Although we may control the environment and pamper ourselves, still we will come to realize that, at any moment, our last breath may go out and never return. How can we be content knowing full well that at best we will be buried?

Many people throughout the world do not even receive such consideration. In Equador there is a public cemetery that systematically milks the Indians of whatever money they may have. Many Indians who live near the capital city have taken to drinking, and somehow they cannot take as much alcohol as the white man. In Quito, almost every day, people die from a heart attack,

This Qur'anic concept, however, is often used by Muslims in a negative way. Allah does not expect a man to perform beyond his capabilities, but He does expect him to perform to the extent of his abilities. We as Muslims, because we take for granted Allah's forgiveness, do not always exert enough effort. Then we use the verse which we have just cited as an excuse for laziness.

We have developed habits which are basically good — they are a part of the total culture — but we abuse them. For example, we often use marriage as a 'spiritual' excuse by quoting the Prophetic tradition, "Marriage is half of the path of Islam." We fail to complete the tradition because the rest is not convenient. The remainder of the tradition says, "...so that one can pay attention to what matters." But we don't like that part, so we omit it. We do the same thing with the Qur'an. And all this has happened because there has been little exertion on our part. We have not suffered. We have been blessed by the bounty and the mercy of Islam, this great gift. But like all gifts, it is not preserved, revived, purified, and respected. If we do not truly and utterly unite with it, its value will be lost. Islam will then become, like all other religions, superficial, social, ceremonial and ritualistic. The responsibility is ours. No one else will come to our rescue. As the Prophet said: "Everyone of you is a shepherd and each is responsible for his flock."

We are forgetting the importance of the inner awakening within us, because the beauty of the outer situation, in material advancement, often distracts from the energy of being aware and watchful. We forget the prophetic tradition which says, "He who knows himself knows his Lord." We neglect the knowledge of our inner self. Why do we do this? If this speaker had a motive in his speech here, then the outcome of it and the transmission of it would be as that motive.

The bounty of Allah is in every situation. His mercy can be found wherever we look. The believer firmly believes in this message. Often he believes blindly until it becomes a reality for him and he is not separate from it. It is not that every now and then he sits down to remember Allah. Rather he as —

Those who are constant at their prayer.

(70:23)

for the city is situated at about 11,000 feet above sea level. Since they drink excessively, many of them are destitute when they die. On the average, it costs the equivalent of $600 to buy a cemetery plot. The Indians are usually able to give a down payment, but in two or three months time they can no longer make the payments. The graves are then bulldozed and sold as new plots. It is a great blessing to be buried by people who have affection for one.

Returning to the subject of grossness and subtlety, we notice that we are born concerned about our immediate environment. We are programmed to unify with it. Unification, known in Arabic as *tawhid*, means to see the cause and effect, to see the interrelationship of the self with the universe. We start with what is immediately in front of us, grouping with objects around us. The child puts things in his or her mouth, trying to connect with them. The act is assimilation, an aspect of *tawhid*, wanting to unify with what the thing is. Soon the child becomes more discriminating as the faculty of reasoning begins to develop. Often, however, the intellect does not evolve. Human beings grow in physical size but still act like children. Size is not necessarily an indicator of inner growth, wisdom and meaning. The normally evolving person moves toward the subtle. If one is protected environmentally, with the right companionship, and sufficient clothes, one should normally seek something higher mentally. This is natural. One wants to know more. Yet people get diverted, distracted and deflected from this goal.

Allah is the goal and the method is remembrance of Him. How do you remember Allah? First by accepting the laws that govern our existence, then by moving higher and higher. The Prophet advises us to know Allah's actions, to know Allah's attributes, and then one may come to know Him.

> Surely We have shown him the way... .
>
> (76:3)

Everyone must determine how to act and do his best:

> Allah does not impose upon any soul but to the extent of its ability.
>
> (2:286)

He becomes fully aware at all times of Allah's mercy:

> He it is Who sends His blessings on you, and (so
> do) His angels that He may bring forth out of utter
> darkness into the light; and He is Merciful to the
> believers.
>
> (33:43)

The believer is always inwardly content because he sees why
the situation has arisen. Outwardly, he may be very discontent
because there is injustice, abuse, ignorance and all the other
things that man encounters. But when was there not injustice?
We must not be romantic about the time of the Prophet. Ibn
'Abbas and several others relate that there were so many verses
of the Qur'an and Prophetic injunctions concerning hypocrisy
that they thought that none of the Companions would be spared
from such a description. We should also reflect upon how the
Prophet died, the confusion and disobedience surrounding him
in the last days of his illness, and the political manoeuvering for
power just after his death. Those of us who truly love the Prophet
will also go through similar experiences because we are his followers.

8

Inner Meaning of the Qur'an

Nothing in existence takes place unless there is a reason behind it. Our scientific endeavours and technical achievements have all progressed because of the search for cause and effect, building up the information base for what is now our contemporary, modern society, with its far-reaching programmes probing further into outer rather than inner space. Whatever we pursue in our intellectual life, using our brain capacity, is based on a sharable pattern that we can understand within the context of a language or a culture. Whenever we are shocked, disappointed, afraid, or uncertain, it is because a discontinuity has taken place in our thought pattern. If someone suddenly begins speaking in a language one cannot understand, there will be an immediate freeze in the communication. So discontinuity is what we do not accept or like, by our innate nature.

The fundamentals in the source-book came down in one instant upon the Prophet of Islam and unfolded outwardly over twenty three years. These two apparently opposing statements are not incompatible, because the Book has always existed. The Book of Creation existed before the creation was made manifest. An analogy is to reflect upon any outer programme. Before we embark on the construction of a house, the design already exists somewhere, maybe in the mind of the potential owner or the architect, and it unfolds in a pattern that is outwardly visible. And so with Qur'an: it is a pattern, a map, like a transparency which one can take and superimpose on any aspect of existence to see it's meaning. It is as if one needs a gradational or topographical presentation which collates the map of life in a fashion that is understandable to us. If the knowledge of the map is alive and available, one will see Reality wherever one looks, and it will never change. Allah says in the Qur'an in *Surat al-Mulk:*

> He who created the seven heavens in one above
> another; you see no incongruity in the creation of
> the Beneficient God; then look again, can you see
> any fault? Then turn back the eye again and again;

> your look shall come back to you confused and
> fatigued.
>
> (67:3-4)

There is no fault in the original design. This does not mean that there is no fault in the situation created by the human element. In other words, the designer's intention is the perfect connectedness of it all, but we are given limited freedom to act. Within that limitation we will bring about injustice. So injustice in this world is our doing, inadvertently. This will continue until we realize that we have no option but to be in submission, to be in Islam, to give in to the decree of the Creator. Once that process has begun, then we have started on the path that was intended for us, by choice.

The Prophet Adam, peace be upon him, had no choice — he was in the Garden. There was nothing other than uniformity so he could only be obedient — he had no other choice. He learned the meaning of disobedience by obediently listening to that vibration called Shaytan. Now here we are in this Reality which is based on duality. We find ourselves born wanting to live forever, seeking friendship, and abhoring enmity, seeking security and fearing insecurity, having varying degrees and different contexts of love and hate. We are all the same. The Qur'an says:

> We created you from one self.
>
> (4:1)

The manifestation of hatred, insecurity, fear or love differs from one person to another, indeed from time to time for the same person. Before breakfast the manifestation of the desire for the person who has awakened hungry is to eat a good breakfast. After breakfast, if he is sensible, the last thing he wants is a second course. We find ourselves in a situation that hinges on duality, and yet there is a thread in it for all of us which we may refer to as mankind or humanity. We are one lot, we are one people, *homosapiens* — there is a common denominator.

Let us now look at the inner meaning of the Qur'an. There cannot be an inner unless there is an outer and the outer is a true reflection of the inner. Therefore, from the Qur'anic point of view, all things in this existence, whether they are material, intellectual or even subtler elements, are interconnected. From this point of view everything is divine, having emanated from the same Divine Source. So truly speaking, there is no such thing as a visible element of our way of life separated from the invisible element.

To put it another way, in reality there is no difference between the traditional and the mystical way of Islam. Where does one end and the other begin? How can you differentiate between the outer and the inner? The outer has an inner reality, and the inner will manifest in the outer realm. An intention will eventually manifest itself in an action. Where is the boundary that prevents that continuum? Where does the atom end and the physical reality of matter begin?

There are interspaces between these systems. As you know, scientists can describe various systems according to different scientific theories. We can describe a gravitational system in detail in the science of physics, but when you come to thermodynamics or the subatomic world, there is another system we can still describe. We know the interrelationships between these systems and yet we cannot define them precisely. So we must refute this separation of the outer and the inner.

Allah says in the Qur'an:

> He is the First and He is the Last. He is the Evident
> and He is the Hidden.
>
> (57:3)

Where is it that He is not? So if we are talking about a unified state, the foundation of all inner sciences, then wherever we begin, we are bound to end up at its opposite. If one begins with outer concern such as the ritual of purification, one will eventually end up with inner concern. If one begins by cleaning the house from the outside, a time will come when the inside will be cared for. And the Qur'an makes this point in one *ayah*, if not in many. The Qur'an says:

> And purify your clothes.
>
> (74:4)

We must understand that the purification of outer garments is superfluous unless one is concerned about the purification of one's body, mind and heart, for they all interconnect. A man is known by how he lives, what he eats, and his immediate environment. The prophetic tradition tells us that one who keeps the company of a people for forty days becomes like them. Inadvertently their characteristics are imbibed.

If one has an inner eye, reflecting upon the outer meaning of the verses of the Qur'an will lead one to their inner meanings. Existence is entirely balanced on opposites — life and death, man and woman, good and bad, sleep and wakefulness, health and disease — and we want at all times to be in the middle. Imbalance results from not being in the middle. Let us examine the virtue known as courage. On one side of courage is cowardice, and on the other is recklessness. Courage is that very fine point right in the middle. Every other virtue is the same — balanced between two extremes. Regarding this, the Qur'an says:

> And we have created you a middle nation.
>
> (2:143)

This nation is the people of unification, people who want to know the truth, and whose Qur'an is every breath of life.

Let us share one short *surah* (chapter) of the Qur'an, *Surat al-Shams* (The Sun), so that we may see how the inner and the outer are totally connected.

> I swear by the sun and its brilliance,
> And the moon when it follows the sun.
>
> (91:1–2)

Allah — Glory, Majesty, and Might are His alone — is reminding us by the effulgence of the sun in the form of an oath, swearing by it. By the radiant sun which gives us warmth and heat. Allah has started by giving us a physical proof of one of the major causes of life on this earth — the sun. By the fact that there is this self-fusing, self-perpetuating light which is the sun. And by the moon which reflects the sun's light.

> And the day when it exposes it,
> And the night when it draws a veil over it.
>
> (91:3–4)

Here Allah reminds us of the other two opposites — day and night.

The description is very beautiful even from a poetic point of view, that this incredible effulgent day suddenly has something thrown over it to hide and cover it. Allah now reveals another pair of opposites to strengthen the oath even further.

> And by the heaven and Him who made it, and by the earth and Him who extended it.
>
> (91:5–6)

And then Allah comes to us:

> And by the self and Him who made it perfect.
>
> (91:7)

A related derivation of the word for self is *nafas* which means 'breath'. We are hanging on air, inhaling and exhaling — again two opposite states, yet we become arrogant and forget this fact. Do we really identify ourselves with these physical forms, walking about!

Allah immediately brings us from the cosmic story to the microcosmic story. We are the reflectors of the macrocosm. The subtle implication, the inner meaning of the verse, is that this self must contain all the double elements that were mentioned in the preceding verses. Its arrangement is *fitrah*, innate, preprogrammed subgenetically from within. That preprogramming develops through stages and time in a contiguous fashion. The root meaning for innate *(fitrah)* is 'to crack'. The child breaks into this world with a cry of despair at being dislodged from the aqueous, contented, mild situation of the preceeding nine months, where it knew only the sound of the mother's heart. Suddenly the child is ejected into a gaseous environment and disconnected from that incredible umbilical situation. Immediately the programmed unfoldment of the self begins. The child is born wanting to connect. The first connection is physical. The first worship is to maintain the body — that is the temple that the child knows innately, and the mother's breast is the object which fulfils that need. In time, if one grows in consciousness, one recognizes that the breast is the earth from which we take our physical sustenance.

> And by the self and Him who made it perfect.
>
> (91:7)

implies that the self has within itself perfection and completeness of the inner and outer, a combination of visible and invisible realities.

Then Allah says:

> Then He inspired it to understand immorality and piety.
>
> (91:8)

He who is pious is aware at times that he is hanging between these two opposites and that at any moment he may slip. Thus he wants to be in such a wakeful state that his inner and outer are completely connected, otherwise he knows he will slip into the abyss, the abyss of suspicion, doubt, inner hatred, or any of the other abysses that we can inwardly suffer from. It could even be the abyss of outer misbehaviour, such as falling asleep behind the wheel of a car for ten seconds in traffic! Piety *(taqwa)* is that perpetual, spontaneous, continuous and natural awareness. The word does not have a dualistic sense. Immorality or decadence, the opposite of piety, takes one far away from reality. Yet how can we know nearness unless we know what is far? There must be recognition of what is far so that we may then, by our own will, seek nearness. Man can sink to a level of decadence and degeneration lower than any other created thing. And yet the Qur'an tells us that the Angels prostrated themselves to the Adamic consciousness.

These Angelic powers or energies are fully programmed in their own channels but we are unable to penetrate them. It is another world to that which we cannot gain full access for our own sake. Think of our own physical world. If we had eyesight good enough to observe all the creational activity going on around us, we would not be able to place things in the middle perspective. Likewise, if we could receive all the other invisible signals that are going on, angelic or otherwise, call them Angels, radar or infra-red or whatever, untestable, unmeasurable, unseeable, untouchable energy waves so to speak — if we were sensitive to all those energy bundles or waves — we would be so encumbered that, in all probability, we would lose our sanity. Right now, around us, there are millions of waves going back and forth. Fortunately, we have been endowed with selective perception and our horizon is limited. Within this limited horizon we can subjectively test and realise the unlimited horizon that contains it.

So, on the one hand, we have immorality and decadence and on the other, piety and complete awareness. The choice is ours. We make that choice according to the degree of our desire for knowledge. The successful one is he who purifies himself.

> He will indeed be successful who makes it grow in purity.
>
> (91:9)

The verbal root of the word for 'succeed' is 'to plough, till, or cultivate'. Success then implies turning over the soil of the self so that it is aerated and soft and then becomes conducive for the growth of success.

The same is true of the heart. The root of 'heart' in Arabic is *qalb*. The verb *qalaba* means 'to turn'. If the heart is attached to a specific thing then that is the limit of cognizance. If the heart turns, however, then it can select what is most appropriate.

Another meaning for the Arabic word which means 'to purify' is 'to increase'. If the impurities of a substance are removed, the substance actually increases, not in quantity but in quality. Also, a derived noun, *zakah*, means charity. Purification of the self is a consequence of giving away and leads to increase. Allah prescribes for us precisely through the example of His Prophet and that of the great beings who followed him, so that we may know, even in the most vulgar circumstances, how to give justly. Within this system nobody is overlooked.

Those who completely and utterly know in themselves that they have no right to own anything in this world, and are at best the guardians of a few things for a short while, are accommodated. Those who think they will take their few possessions to the grave must also be accommodated. All are Allah's creation.

Regarding the purity of the self and the inner and outer, we can never know anyone's heart. No one has the right to do so. The prime example is from the Battle of Badr, when the Muslims were being attacked, and someone was under Zayd's sword. As he was about to slay the man with his sword, the man shouted out "There is no god but Allah." Zayd then killed him. The blessed Prophet told Zayd: "You have killed a Muslim." Zayd said: "He was a liar." The Prophet answered: "And do you know what was in his heart?"

We can only judge one another by our outer behaviour. We cannot question another's intentions, only his actions. If we purify the outer and continue, eventually we will end up connected with the inner. This will save us a lot of dissipated energy. If one knows what one wants and is sincere about it, one is happy and pure without expectations. If one's intention is free from arrogance or any other lower tendency, then most of one's energy is preserved. Clarity, efficiency and success are the promised results.

> And he will certainly fail who buries it.
>
> (91:10)

We must not conceal the truth that within us lies the potentiality of the best and the worst. Within us lies arrogance, fearfulness, forgetfulness, and selfishness, and also generosity, patience and sacrifice.

Now the *surah* shows us how, on an individual level, if we do not awaken and rise inwardly towards unity, we will be destroyed even as nations are destroyed. So the Qur'an gives us the example in the next verses:

> The people of Thamud denied the truth by their
> unrestrained actions,
> when the most unfortunate of them broke forth
> with mischief.
>
> (91:11–12)

Allah calls our attention to the people of Thamud, a great nation, a great civilization. They followed the worst amongst them, those who were most arrogant. Allah says in the Qur'an that when the time has come for a town, village or culture to be destroyed, the most arrogant and villainous amongst them will become their leaders. The truth will then prevail against them and they will be destroyed.

> So the Messenger of Allah said to them: This is
> Allah's she-camel, so give her drink.
>
> (91:13)

Allah says: No people, no civilization, no culture will be destroyed without first being warned as to the purpose of their existence so that they may live honourably, nobly and fully, manufacturing in this life the key to the Garden. If they struggle outwardly to do their best, inwardly they will be totally content. Outwardly, they will never be content because there is always something to be done. One of the main names of Allah is *Rabb*. *Rabb* is He who raises or brings up fully. The people of Thamud were interested in earth-shattering, miraculous events, so they asked the prophet Salih, who said: "I will ask Allah to aid me with a miracle, but then you must abide by the rules." They consented, so a she-camel appeared from the rocks. The prophet Salih told them: "There are certain rules regarding this she-camel. One day she is to drink water and the next day you may drink. And you must not molest her, otherwise, you will be destroyed." The people were shocked by this event.

Many of the prophets coupled their natural, simple messages to mankind with a miracle in order to attract the attention of those people who were not yet as sophisticated intellectually as we are today. They needed a jolt. In the case of the Seal of the Prophets, the Prophet Muhammad, mankind had reached a point in development where there was no need for that outer jolt. The pronouncement of truth itself was the greatest of all miracles.

> But they called him a liar and slaughtered her,
> therefore their Lord crushed them for their sin and
> levelled them.
>
> (91:14)

They denied the truth, even when there was a visible, physical miracle. Something came from the unseen to the seen, and they denied and acted against it, therefore they were destroyed.

> And He fears not its consequence.
>
> (91:15)

Allah is not concerned about what we may consider to be an appropriate outcome. This means that it is of no consequence if a whole nation or nations are destroyed in order to restore equilibrium. And Allah says in the Qur'an:

> And you shall not find any change in the course of Allah.
>
> (33:62)

Illness is a manifestation of mercy, so that one's physical balance is restored, so that one seeks help, cognizance and reasoning to bring oneself back to physical balance. Then the body, which is the container of that subtle reality, the spirit, is fit to contain the spirit. The body is basically the vehicle upon which the spirit rides during it's journey on earth, the few years of upbringing to prepare the spirit to inhabit, once again, the infinite reality from which it came. If the body is not fit, the inner subtler aspect cannot be fit. Therefore, our priority starts from the outer. We must be fairly well physically and content mentally so that we are balanced. Then we can reflect the true light within us, taking from reality what is useful and beneficial. From this balanced state we can then study branches of science which are analytical and divisive. Such studies require an observer and an observed. That is another system, one of causality with its laws and conditions. And it is important as part of our existence.

In a sense, we are born deficient in order to be able to develop our scientific, causal attitude. But this aspect of ourselves is encompassed within another reality which possesses a unifying factor. If we do not allow our causal knowledge to operate in conjunction with this unifying factor, then we will merely have a great deal of outer knowledge but no inner vision.

We find in nature that a child's simple, physical disposition is accepted, because all he understands is physical unification. When an older person, however, possesses no inner wisdom or sprituality we tend to dismiss him. In our eastern societies the youngsters traditionally kept company with the elders for this was the right balance. The child physically has few limits, where as the old man is physically limited but inwardly almost limitless, because he is approaching the Limitless. The two are in the right balance. Increasingly in western socieits, the older people are shunned, put away in old people's homes. They do not see children, it is a separatist or compartmentalised society. I am not condemning the West or upholding the East, for the East is now becoming like the West. What matters is that everything must be in its rightful place.

As we cannot allow our causal knowledge to operate without unific knowledge, so we cannot exclude causal knowledge, for the causal realm is the realm of Allah's means. Let us examine an Islamic tradition about the Prophet Musa. On one occasion he was very ill, and refused to take medicine from the Jewish doctors because he was so disgusted with them. He made a vow that he would only accept Allah's direct intercession, for he was in direct communication with Allah. The doctors felt sorry for him and were dimly aware of how much trouble they had caused him, so they came with their medicines, but he refused. He became increasingly ill and was on the verge of death when he asked Allah: "Oh Allah! What shall I do? I was depending on you." Allah answered him saying: "Just because you are near to Me, do you expect Me to abrogate the means of My wisdom? Those who came to you are My means." So Musa accepted the help of the doctors.

This is how Allah unifies outwardly. This is how Allah softens people's hearts towards each other. If we do not recognize the means, we will never recognize the source behind the means. Our Prophet says: "If you do not thank those who have given you something, you have not thanked the real Giver." So we must thank Allah for giving us this incredible gift called life, which manifests in so many lives and yet is one life. We must thank Allah for having given us the opportunity to share amongst ourselves. We must ask Allah to give us the opportunity to ignite that inner flame whose lamp already exists within us, for He says:

> The heavens and earth do not contain Me, but the
> heart of a trusting believer contains Me.

9

Keys to the Kingdom

Commentary on *Surat al-Mulk*

Part I

As we all know, each *ayah* of the Qur'an had a specific reason for which it came during the Prophet's life-time. If the *ayats* do not have reasons and meanings which are valid for the time in which we live, then we may as well consider the *ayats* useless. If, for instance, we say *Surah Abu Lahab* which is about Abu Lahab, a contemporary of the Prophet, does that mean that there have not been others like Abu Lahab since the Prophet?

Along with history of the revelation of the *ayats*, there is another matter which is very important, and that is the knowledge of those *ayats* which were abrogated and those which abrogate. But these two aspects of the Qur'anic science are best left to the scholars. With the short time at our disposal it is best to dive into the Qur'an in such a fashion that it is immediately usable as a practical manual even without much knowledge of Arabic.

In order to display what I mean, *Surat al-Mulk* has been chosen. Allah says in the first *ayah:*

> Blessed is He in Whose hand is the Kingdom, and
> He has power over all things.
>
> (67:1)

In other words, 'Exalted be He in whose hands is all sovereignty.' *Mulk*, meaning kingdom, is anything that is owned, anything that can be discerned. It may designate something physical or it may represent a concept such as sovereignty. *Mulk* is from the verb *malaka* which means 'to have power, to control, to possess'. So, whatever you possess, for instance your life, is *mulk*. Along with the thing possessed is implied its value. Generally speaking, *mulk* implies a piece of land or a house because this is the most obvious possession.

The Qur'an says *tabaraka*. *Mubarak*, a derivative of *tabaraka*, is that which is blessed. Recognizing His blessedness and His mercy and that the entire Creation is in His hands means that I recognize my nothingness. The phrase 'the hands of Allah' implies action, manifestation, and visibility. As you know we have two hands and, in our traditions the right is for enjoying what is correct while the left is for forbidding the wrong. In conformity with that, we encourage our children to eat with their right hands.

Our life and every life is His. The Qur'an tells us the most important trade is the selling of ourselves to Allah. If we give ourselves up to Him, then whatever problem that remains is Allah's. Having truly surrendered ourselves, we recognize that all is in Allah's hand. The reality of the situation is that we are in-time while He is not. Time is encapsulated by Him. Through this limitation we have to discover the Unlimited. This means that we must leave the possibility open for anything to happen. What we call a miracle is actually an event about which we are completely ignorant. It is unseen to us but, as far as Allah is concerned, the unseen and the seen are connected. For us, because we are caught within time, the seen and the unseen are separated.

> He is the knower of the Unseen and the Knower
> of witnessing.
>
> (6:73)

We recognize that He is All-Powerful over all things, but sometimes this leades us to rationalize that Allah will change whatever we wish to be changed without any effort on our part.

Every event is according to perfect laws. If it were not so, there would be chaos and no mercy. If every one of us were born with a defect causing our hearts to stop for twenty seconds, can you imagine what chaos we would experience? We want to know if our health is going to last and we are concerned about the immediate future because we hope to unify our intentions with our actions. We want *tawhid* (unification). We love the One and only One, the One on whom all depend, but we do not know Muhammad, the Prophet of Allah. Many people say "There is no god but God," and accept this *ayah*. But this is not enough.

If they do not move from "There is no god but God" to "Muhammad is the Prophet of Allah," and find the keys to the Muhammadi way, it is not good enough. Having accepted that Allah is All-Powerful over all things, it is our duty to unify our destiny with His will. If that unification occurs, then we are safe in the house of Faith.

Allah's will manifests itself in the consensus of opinion. If all of us here were to want goodness, goodness would prevail. But if the majority of us wanted something rotten and hypocritical, and only one person wanted goodness, what would prevail? It is obvious that the one desiring good would be overpowered. He would be a believer amongst disbelievers or hypocrites. Then it would be his duty to try to change the situation, failing which, he should do the next best thing, which is to leave. Even a prophet of Allah would be distressed by an environment of unbelief. The Prophet Moses was not spared the afflictions of the plague of blood. Similarly, during the Battle of Uhud, the blessed Prophet Muhammad was not protected from the laws of gravity which guided the arrow to his teeth. These events occurred within Allah's laws. While the Prophet's inward self recognized the Perfection of Allah, and therefore was content with the loss that the Muslims suffered, his outward self wanted to continue fighting in order to save them. Yet the two aspects of his being were totally united. Inwardly, he was content with the decree of Allah; outwardly, he was a slave of Allah. "Allah is All-Powerful over all things." We see the signs of this truth everywhere, although we are remote from this glorious reality. The Muhammadi way is to do our best at each instant according to our capacities and to move on. The rest is Allah's business.

> Who created death and life that he may try you —
> which of you is best in deeds; and He is the
> Mighty, the Forgiving.
>
> (67:2)

The *Surah* began with "Glory be to the One Who has it all," that is, He has all of the Kingdom, the *mulk*. Now Allah points out a subtlety concerning the manifestation of His Glory in the Creation. Look at the Qur'an. We have to question it in order to fully comprehend what it is offering. We have to ask why He put *mawt* (death) before *hayat* (life) in His statement: "Who created death and life."

One of the many ways of approaching an answer to this question is to begin with the premise that the Creation has a purpose. If you were trying to design something you would first form a model or an idea of it in its completion. You would then move towards meeting your goal within a specific time. Concerning our own end, it is death, and it is towards that that we are all working.

In a sense, we are programmed to fear death. While the believer has it always in front of him, the unbeliever seeks to keep it behind him so that he may deny it. When Allah says: "He created death," He means to indicate that our lives begin at what is ultimately going to happen to us, which is death. It means that we are as good as our state when we leave this world. Allah promises that this is what will ultimately count.

One of the meanings of *bala* (to try) is 'to make something old'. It means 'to test'. We see, therefore, that the ageing process is a series of tests to prepare us for the ultimate end. Afflictions are not against us, but rather for us. Allah tests us so that we may acquire discrimination which will give us the appreciation and knowledge that will cause us to grow worthy of our origin which is the Command of Allah. Allah says:

> And they ask you about the soul. Say: the soul is
> one of the commands of my Lord, and you are not
> given aught of knowledge but a little.
>
> (17:85)

With sound discrimination we would be worthy of being called *Bani Adam* (the sons of Adam). We would know what is right and what is not, recognizing what is lasting and what is not. Once we have put our priorities in order, we will become men of wisdom and intellect *('aql)*. The head gear of the Arabs is called the *'aqal* a word related to *'aql*. Before the Cadillacs overcame the camels in the Arab world it had another function. It was tied round the legs of the camel to make him sit. *'Aqala* means to 'become tranquil, still'. In Arabic you say *'iql!* (Be

quiet! Sit down!) By implication we see that the faculty of tether-
ing originates within us. If agitation ceases, consciousness arises.
'*Aql* is generally translated as 'mind' or 'thought'. Allah says in
a *Hadith Qudsi:*"One of the first things I created was '*Aql*."

"Which of you is best in deeds?" How do we discriminate
between actions except by what gives rise to consciousness
through the '*aql?* The worth of an action is according to the
purity of its intention. If the intention behind our action were
service to Allah, then we would permit the outcome of the action
to fall completely into Allah's hands. Although our judgement
may have been wrong in the application of the action, still, Allah
will take care of our intention. If our intention was correct, He
will save us. He will determine:

> Which of you is best in deeds; and He is the Mighty,
> the Forgiving.
>
> (67:2)

'*Aziz* (Mighty) is one of the names of Allah and means 'Precious'. Often, when Allah's attributes are mentioned at the end
of an *ayah*, they reveal its meaning. '*Aziz* here refers to the Creator
of death and life which are most precious to us.

Ghafur is the forgiver of our actions. *Ghafara* in Arabic means
'to protect, to cover'. *Ghafara* and *kafara* mean almost the same
thing in an outer sense. *Kafara* is 'to cover, wrap with something'.
A *kafir* is someone who 'denies, covers up, denies the mercy of
Allah'. *Ghafara* means to cover faults. We ask Allah for *ghufran,*
His covering of our faults.

> Who creatd the seven heavens one above another;
> you see no incongruity in the creation of the Bene-
> ficent God; then look again, can you see any fault?
>
> (67:3)

In the first *ayah* we were informed that the entire Creation is
Allah's territory, the *mulk*. In the second *ayah* we are given a
short description of the Creator. A *Hadith Qudsi* says: "I was a
hidden treasure and I wanted to be known so I created." The
dispersion or separateness apparent in the creation is only to

spur us on to recognizing His Oneness. The secret of the Oneness is hidden within what appears to be separateness. Allah says: "I am closer to you than your jugular vein." Wherever you look is the face of Allah — Wherever you look there is Oneness. The Qur'an says:

> O man! Surely you must strive (to attain) to your
> Lord, a hard striving until you meet Him.
>
> (84:6)

Where do you go to attain the vision of oneness but "(the One) Who created the seven heavens... ."

This *ayah* of *Surat al-Mulk* is a more detailed description of the expansiveness of the Creator's manifestation and can be viewed in many ways. According to Islamic science, there are outward seven heavens and seven inward heavens. The present day science of physics describes the atom as containing electrons which occupy seven energy levels. Linguistically, the Arabic language implies by the word 'seven', 'many'.

Tabaq means 'layer upon layer'. The implecation is that there are layers one on top of the other, all intimately connected. In one sense this may be interpreted to mean a hierarchy of levels beginning at the grossly physical extending to the less physical and subtle. For example, the air which surrounds our planet is found to be most dense at the surface and most subtle as we leave the gravitational pull of the earth.

Within this *ayah* we are given an aspect of the Mercy of Allah. "You do not see in the creation of the Merciful (*Rahman*) any deviation, any imperfection." *Tafawut* means 'incongruency' or 'deviation, and comes from the verb *fata* which means 'to escape'. You will never see such a state of affairs in the creation. It is perfect from whichever direction you look at it. If you ever suspect that there may be some incongruity in the events that have taken place within your life, look back at what happened, you will find it was perfect — even though you may not have had success. In whatever happned there was mercy in it for you.

Know that whatever was taken away from you can be replaced by something as good or better. From the child in the womb is taken away the wonderful protectiveness and security. The sec-

urity is robbed from him in order that he may grow to witness
this world in its magnificence and perfection. Contemplation on
Allah is not possible without giving up something. You have to
give up something to obtain something else. It is mathematical,
a perfect balance.

Futur is 'a fissure', 'a crack', and comes from *fatara* which
means 'to crack, or to split'. Would we ever expect to find a
crack or discontinuity within this creation? If we do see any
discontinuities in the creation, it is because we are discontinuous
and cracked within ourselves. Then we are discontinuous on our
path of knowledge of Allah.

One of the many courtesies we practise in our approach to
the Qur'an is the reciting of the phrase "I seek protection with
Allah from the accursed Shaytan." The development of our discrimination begins by our recognition of what is not correct. We
know, in our existential life, what is not right before we know
what is right.

Shatana the root of Shaytan in Arabic means 'to be far'. We
do not wish to be near what will cause us to be far from Allah.
If it were not for our appreciation of being distant, we would
not appreciate being near. If it were not for the fact that we have
suffered from falsehood, we would not be able to approach the
truth. Excluding what is not, as expressed by '*"la ilaha"*, is the
right form of courtesy. In this way discrimination and *'aql*
(reasoning) grows, the faculty of higher consciousness is fed.

Another courtesy shown towards the Qur'an is keeping oneself
in ritual purity (i.e. in *wudu'*). If the beginning is right then the
end will be right; if the beginning is wrong then the end will be
wrong. We must ask ourselves 'Is our ablution real? Have we
washed off all bad actions. Given up everything that the left
hand does and made sure that the right hand will do what it is
supposed to do? Have we wiped out all the senses?' Shaykh
al-Alawi, who is one of our great masters, explains quite a number
of the inner meanings of *wudu'*. There are many traditions indi-
cating the inner meanings of our outer actions.

If we do not unify the inner and the outer, we shall miss the
sweetest, deepest nectar. According to many great men of knowledge and reality, the *ayah* "In the Name of Allah, the Beneficent,

the Merciful" belongs to every *surah* except one. "In the Name of Allah, the Beneficent, the Merciful" should never be neglected because it is the most important, the most blessed, the most perfect, the most loved *ayah*. Each *"Bismillahi Rahmani Rahim"* is specific to its *surah*. There are many men of *'ilm* (knowledge) who say that if, while performing the prayer, one recites *"Bismillahi Rahmani Rahim"* without already having chosen the *surah* one is about to read, the prayer is not correct. *"Bismillahi Rahmani Rahim"*, as the first *ayah* of *Surat al-Mulk*, means that *barakah* (blessedness) is in the hand of the One and Only Controller. It means here that it is the decree of Allah that "Blessed is He in Whose hand is the kingdom".

An Arabic word is usually formed of a three-consonant cluster. That cluster will form many adjectives, verbs and nouns which sound similar yet have specific meanings. For example, *wafa*. When an Arab hears the word, he immediately associates it with the concept which in English would mean 'loyalty, honesty' etc. But when *wafat* is heard, the concept of 'death' comes to his mind. The many other words related to *wafa* when conceived together act as a kaleidoscope which creates new higher-order meanings, serving to enhance the specific word and its meaning.

When we translate the Qur'an, we must give each word a specific meaning according to the situation. At first the heart should remain open to the reality of the field of *tawhid*, the unified field, picking up all of the vibrations of the words closely related to it. At last, seeing the panorama of interrelated meanings, it should anchor itself on one specific meaning, already established within our traditions.

We cannot do *ta'wil* (interpretation) in our own way. It is inspired and the activity of the Inspired Self is very dangerous. *Nafs al-ammarah* (the Commanding Self), which is considered a lower form of self, is in fact easier to overcome. The Inspired Self is the heart of an artist. It is attractive because it projects the impression of having freedom, but it is dangerous and may lead to disaster. The Commanding Self and the Self-Accusing Self are terrible but they are easy to identify. Typically, they would say, 'I will not budge'. If they are not appealed to intellectually, spiritually, mentally, they will not give in. Whereas the Inspired Self says, 'Never mind, why not, we are open minded, etc.' It is the worst type of self, especially where teaching is concerned. It is an arrogant, egotistical self, possessing no discipline. The man who is under the sway of the Inspired Self, when he takes to the path, has no discipline and is like jelly. For this reason we cannot do our own interpretation, following our own inspirations. We let our hearts wander but in the end we must anchor ourselves. The Qur'an addresses the human being as follows:

> O soul that art at rest!
>
> (89:27)

The Qur'an does not address the Inspired Self.

Ism (name) in the *ayah "Bismillahi Rahmani Rahim"* leads the mind of a person, who is familiar with Arabic, in the direction of another word, *sama,* which means 'higher'. *Ism* specifically means 'that which points towards a direction, a name, a label'. The label of a thing is not the thing. Everything in this existence points towards its Creator and, therefore, how many names has Allah? Where is it that Allah's name is not, because where is it that Allah is not? When we say, "In the Name of Allah, the Beneficent, the Merciful", we mean, 'By the permission, by the direction, by the pointer which can be recognized through His beneficence and mercy.'

Allah is *Ism al-Jalal* (the Majestic Name). He is pure and cannot be described because no sooner does the consciousness become conscious of something than the thing conceived becomes impure. No sooner do we think of an attribute but that attribute will be coloured by time and place. When we say, "In the Name of Allah" it must point necessarily in a particular direction.

> In the Name of Allah, the Beneficent, the Merciful.
> Say: He, Allah, is One.
>
> (112:1)

"Bismillahi Rahmani Rahim" at the beginning of *Surat al-Ikhlas* means 'By the power of life and discrimination that is in us to say the truth' which is *"Allahu Ahad* (Allah is One)." Every decla-

ration of "In the Name of Allah" has its own specific meaning: it is part of a *surah* and cannot be separated from it. It is the decree of Allah that this is the way it is, whether we like it or not.

> Blessed is He in Whose Hand is the kingdom.
>
> (67:1)

When *"Bismillah"* is used at the beginning of *Surah al-Mulk* it means, 'The name of Allah is stamped on all of His creation, on all of his *mulk* (kingdom).'

As a summary of the three *ayats* of *Surat al-Mulk* we have covered, we can say that the first *ayah* is an acknowledgement of the Mercy of Allah and that He is in control. "He has power over all things." Then the creation is informed that it is He "Who created death and life." Death is the set target from life's inception. We have come into this world in order to find its opposite. All knowledge of existence, as we know, hinges on the recognition of opposites. We cannot recognize wakefulness unless we sleep, knowledge unless we are ignorant, right unless we have understood the meaning of wrong within us. We cannot recognize the value of good health unless we have suffered from ill health. The access to one attribute is through its opposite. It is well known that everything which goes beyond its boundary becomes its opposite. If we are completely divested for Allah's sake, we will become ultimately rich by Allah. If we want something we have to go to its opposite. If we want to rule, we have to be willing to be ruled over. But first we have to know how to rule ourselves. Ultimately, we should have no wish or desire for ourselves, otherwise, we would not be qualified to rule. The Prophet appointed Usamah, the youngest of his companions to command the Muslim army and take control of a country. There were other companions who were much older, wiser and much more knowledgeable. One of them came to the Prophet to say that he was better qualified than the young Usamah. But the Prophet said: "You may well be better qualified; you both have many similar qualities, but he has one which you do not. He does not want to rule and you do."

If a person wishes to be a successful ruler, one of the necessary qualifications is its opposite, not wanting to rule, that is, not

wanting to rule for ourselves but for Allah. We will rule to bring
joy, to open other people's hearts. By taking advantage of the
opportunity in this life to attain tranquillity of the heart, stability
of the system, a moment of emptiness, we will move inward
toward the discovery of the inner cosmos. Allah says:

> So when you are free still toil.
>
> (94:7)

In other words, we should remain steadfast and expand our
hearts.

Imam 'Ali has said the following:

> "Your remedy is within you but you don't know
> it.
> "Your illness is self-inflicted but you do not see it.
> "And you are the evident book. By its signs
> appears what is hidden.
> "And you imagine yourself a tiny planet or a
> tiny entity and in you is folded up the entire cos-
> mos."

What the Imam is saying becomes romantic pseudo-Sufism if
we are not careful. We must start correctly, properly, and with
the right courtesy. We cannot jump ahead to gain inner delights
without first attending to outer responsibilities. Everything has
its turn. The Prophet said: "The path, in its entirety, is courtesy."
Our courtesy towards the Qur'an, towards these *ayats*, is to take
what comes out of them clearly and with cause and then to pray
for greater, deeper clarity which will manifest the connection
between the outer and the inner.

Allah's Creation, whose purpose is for man to come to know
Him, is based upon various layers, manifestations or stages which
have no separation between them. Each stage is part of a continuum. There is nothing in it that we can improve upon because
it is based on a perfect oneness existing in non-timeness. Allah
says:

> Wonderful Originator of the heavens and earth,
> and when He decrees an affair, He only says to it,
> Be, so there it is.
>
> (2:117)

The creation of the world is not a clumsy act put together by in-time beings such as men, rather it is a perfection created by Allah who exists in non-time.

The next *ayah of Surat al-Mulk* is a challenge to Allah's creatures.

> Then turn back the eye again and again; your look
> shall come back to you confused and fatigued.
> (67:4)

There are many different interpretations of this *ayah*. If we spend time on it, we will discover them for ourselves. Some of them we may be able to reveal to others, some of them we may not be licensed to. We are not certain of our inspirations. How do you know if they are absolute in truth? Occasionally we receive openings, but it is discourteous to inflict them upon others.

Very recently, a man of great knowledge warned me that because he had had a certain vision, such and such a situation might arise. Desiring to maintain personal tranquillity, safety and health, all prerequisites for witnessing the cosmic balance, I heeded his warning. But in doing so, I found myself lacking in courtesy. I was admitting that there was nothing that I could do and therefore I was being negative. Besides, it was possible that his vision was not true and was the result of bad indigestion. We do not know. Imam 'Ali said: "Enough of that knowledge (inspirational knowledge) does not exist and the little of it that you receive will be of no use to you."

I have yet to find a master who is absolutely certain of his visions. Still, if I see something about someone and I can do something to help him or her, then it is my duty to do so. Suppose I have a dream that a person is walking and then falls into a well. It would be my duty to come to him quietly and walk beside him to assure him, when we get to that well, that I am there with him to guide him to the other side. I may find that there was no well at all. It was only my own imagination.

So you can see, we cannot do our own interpretation of the Qur'an guided by inspiration. We must be careful and courteous. The most we can say about each of the openings that we do have concerning the Qur'an is that it is one opinion. If linguistically and traditionally there is nothing wrong with our interpre-

tation — nobody has objected to it — and it fits into what the
rest of the Qur'an says, then you may conclude that you have
come upon one way of looking at the meaning of the Qur'an.
Many of the interpreters of the Qur'an pay attention to the outer
surface only. Explaining the Qur'an at a superficial level is safe,
but we want more than a superficial understanding. We are
greedy for knowledge. We must ask Allah to give us the right
qualifications because we have to tread gently and be willing to
withdraw our foot at any time. It is Allah's business, Allah's
knowledge, Allah's model. We have to treat it with the greatest
deference.

'Return the sight twice' is a challenge. We have looked at the
existence and contemplated. If we are Believers, it is not possible
for us to look back for another moment without concluding that
the creation is in a perfect balance. The events of creation may
not be perfect for our pocketbooks or our relationships with our
sons but that is because we have had an objective not in line
with the overall destiny of creation. We may have been in a state
of ignorance *(jahal)* or we may have been clumsy. When we
decided to build a high-rise building, we may not have known
that half a dozen other companies were doing exactly the same
thing. Even though we are very pious and our actions were
dedicated to Allah, we may still find, after finishing the building,
that we have many debts, an empty building, and the bank
manager chasing us. Can we blame Allah? If our actions were
pure and simple *fi-sabilillah* (completely in the way of Allah),
then why should we care? It is Allah's business. Often, of course,
this is not the case; we did not act purely for Allah. This matter
is very subtle because we are usually not aware of our own inner
motives.

When we 'turn back the eye again and again' we have the
chance of not projecting ourselves, thereby having a better opportunity of seeing the perfection of creation and its cause and effect.

Looking back, the believer finds the perfect hand behind all
events and so is able to take immediate cybernetic remedial
action to get back into synchronization. It is to Allah's laws that
we are connected and subjected. Within a small arena we have
the ability to act freely. If the two are not enmeshed in total

harmony along the conveyor belt called time, then sparks fly and then, of course, we blame our loss on someone else.

"...Your look shall come back to you confused... ." If we see imperfection, it is because our vision is imperfect. The disorder that we see is our own. Looking back again and again gives us the possibility of rectifying our interpretation. This is why the *hadith* says, "The believer will not be bitten from the same hole twice." Committing the same mistake twice, as all of us do, indicates that our faith is faulty. Faith has degrees. Where does it end? Wherever there is a fault in our faith, we will tend to fall into it repeatedly because the believer trusts that all is well. But on the other hand, if he trusts that all is well, and his trust is well placed, all will be well. For the believer there is no way out, he is caught. Without complaint, he does whatever is necessary with unified sight, intention and action. The believer is not negative nor does he complain. He is not passive towards his environment like the television viewer.

> Then turn back the eye again and again; your look
> shall come back to you confused and fatigued.
> (67:4)

The meaning of this *ayah* is that the being who tries to see a fault in the creation will not be able to, rather he will become exhausted, without success. Still our common experience leads us to believe that if we want to find fault with the Creation, we will. If we want to find fault with a people, no matter who they are, we will find it because perfection belongs only to Allah. Likewise, if we want to find goodness in a person, we will find it. If we are looking for people of sound heart, we will find people who are kind-hearted. Even in the worst criminal, there is some goodness. Someone who has killed five hundred people may occasionally show kindness towards a cat.

Allah says:

> O man! Surely you must strive (to attain) to your
> Lord, a hard striving until you meet Him.
> (84:6)

We will toil in this life. But often, because we are not on a path,
our toil is merely chasing our own tail in circles. Our efforts may
not be on the *sirat al-mustaqim,* the straight path, the path of
righteousness. The definition of a straight line is that which is
the shortest distance between two points. We imagine there are
two points, Allah and ourselves. The man of real insight will
change his view of the two points so that they are lined up on
a straight line towards the Ka'bah. He will no longer see two
points but one. In that way he will see nothing other than the
One. When we change our attitude we will see the One, and we
will be reborn. Then we shall be like toddlers when they begin
to become aware of their ignorance; the more we see, the more
we know we have not seen. Then all we shall say is:

> There is no god but God, and Muhammad is the
> Messenger of Allah.

and pray that Allah will give us a situation in which we can
share and care and be responsible. The difference between *kufr*
(the denial of truth) and Islam is that in the *kafir* system the
unbeliever asks, 'What is my right, what is my right?' While in
the Islamic system the Muslim asks, 'What is my responsibility?'
The Muslim prays, 'May Allah increase my responsibility so
that I may have no time to increase my ego and arrogance.'

10

Praising the Lord of Creation

Commentary on *Surat al-Mulk*
Part II

Allah's creation has come from oblivion, from a point of non-descriptiveness. In other words, it has come from an eternal void. From this void it exploded and is still expanding. At the proper time that expansion will stop. That will be the first call, as the Qur'an describes it.

The beginning of the expansion of creation has been compared to jelling around what we call a building block. But the more we search to find the building block, the more emptiness we encounter. Ultimately through science we come to the same notion that is described in the Qur'an, that the creation is built upon opposites — there is a seen and an unseen. The unseen might be called the black hole, a phenomenon made popular by modern science.

The exploding, expanding cosmos is an event we have undergone in the womb before our birth. We are duplicating the cosmic story. On a cellular level, our cells are exploding: growing up, reaching a point of maturity, and then declining to death. Likewise, the universe is reaching a point of maturity; it will also decline and collapse ushering in the Second Call, the Second Shout, on the Day of Reckoning. The Afterlife creates the reverse of this waveband, this life. Imagine a wave that is created in a pool. As it travels towards the edge of the pool, it represents this life; once it strikes the poolside and bounces back it represents the next life. Everything which you see here in this life, according to our tradition, according to the Qur'an, will be reversed in the next life. What we hide now will be evident, will be *suhufun manshurah* (pages spread out) in the next life. Our inner will become our outer. Everybody will have a halo, so to speak, of his or her former body. We will recognize each other through the heart by what each has inscribed upon his self in this life through his actions, thoughts and intentions.

> And certainly We have adorned this lower heaven
> with lamps and We have made these missiles for
> the Shaytans, and We have prepared for them the
> chastisement of burning.
>
> (67:5)

This world of ours is the melting pot where deviation occurs. In the early period of creational development there was a great deal of discord. After a time, the energies became more and more stable, the earth cooled. The lowest of all, water, became the substance upon which the throne or dominion of Allah (*'arsh*) settled. There is nothing more degraded than water: it is the smallest atom, hydrogen, oxidized by oxygen. Degrading a substance in this existence usually requires oxidation: it is the substance's final collapse. Anything oxidized is actually recycled. Hydrogen oxidized is degraded to the lowest of all lows. And the entire world is based on that. In this lowest of heavens there are numerous possibilities for Shaytan, or for us acting as instruments of Shaytan, to abuse seen and unseen powers.

We are informed that if we do not behave ourselves properly in this lowest heaven we will receive the "chastisement of the burning fire" (22:4), of which there are levels. There is a small *Qiyamah* (Day of Reckoning) and there is a big *Qiyamah*. When it is mentioned in the Qur'an that there is "the Great Fire" (87:12), it is implied that there is also a Small Fire (*al-nar al-sughra*). We all know the sensation of fire. Unfortunately, we have also had occasion to experience the bitterness of an inner fire of anger, jealousy, envy and hatred. Sometimes the inner fire is good and blessed; such as in the case of being angry with injustice, ignorance and anything that is out of line with Allah's laws. Such anger is good but, nevertheless, still anger. It can spur one to positive action or it can result in an ulcer.

We are given many glimpses of the Fire and the Garden in the Qur'an. About the Garden of the next life the Qur'an says:

> And whoever believes in Allah and does good deeds
> He will cause him to enter gardens beneath which
> rivers flow, to abide therein forever.
>
> (65:11)

We do not know how the rivers are fed because they are allegorical and exist within the context of a parable *(mithal)*.

All of creation is worshipping *al-Latif* (the Subtle One):

> Whatever is in the heavens and the earth declares
> the glory of Allah, and He is the Mighty, the Wise.
>
> (57:1)

We have to call upon the *Latif* for everything. The invocation *(dhikr)* of "*Ya Latif*" (O Subtle One) is a very important one, especially for the Chisti Sufis, as well as for many other *turuq* (paths of worship in Islam). The path of worship cannot be trodden except through the help of the Subtle. Subtlety, in the physical sense, means making something which is solid, fluid. For example, we mix the earth with water in order to establish an alchemical situation that will induce a seed to germinate and later bear fruit. We have to appeal to the Subtle at all times.

We are programmed to move from the gross *(kathif)* to the Subtle *(al-Latif)* irrespective of what we do. Though you may have a good home, wife, children, the aspiration towards that which fosters the intellect to find self-satisfaction does not die. Social psychologists claim there is a hierarchy of self-actualization. As Muslims we see that man moves towards greater subtlety, naturally, and the perception of this does not require the elaborate theories of modern psychology. We are all veering towards Allah, towards His Glorious Names *(al-Asma al-Husna)*. We wish to take on the attributes of *al-Basit* (the Expander), *al-Qabid* (the Constricter), *al-Rafi* (the Bearer). But if we do not have the right courtesy towards these attributes we become demi-gods, wanting to play the role of the Giver, the Taker, the Powerful, the Knowing. We all want Allah and His attributes. Allah says:

> Surely We have shown him the way: he may be
> thankful or unthankful.
>
> (76:3)

Concerning our situation in this life, we are either thankful or unthankful. If we are in the state of gratitude *(shukr)*, we are

content. When we are in this state, we are able to live in the
present. If we are somewhere else, not present, our projections
and imagination dissipate our energies.

The lower heaven is the melting pot to test our mettle. Just
as a gold coin is tested to show its metal, so are we tested by
Allah to prove our worth. The trial *(fitnah)* here on earth will
reveal whether or not we shall rise to our origin and heritage,
prepared for its finality, for ourselves, by ourselves. The trials
and temptations in this life are a part of a cybernetic system
which the self perfects as it moves through experiences and time.
Constantly we are caught, unveiled, revealed to ourselves.

Performing a good action enables us to see our intention. The
Qur'an says we may do it either openly or secretly. So how is it
to be performed? If our *nafs*, the self, prefers to keep it a secret,
we should do the reverse, in order to disappoint the self. At
other times, the self may be completely neutral so that performing
a good action openly would be a good example to others even
though inwardly we see ourselves as showing off. So, this is the
state of the heavens we inhabit. This is the condition of the
creational reality at the physical level.

> And for those who disbelieve in their Lord is the
> doom of Hell, and evil is the resort.
>
> (67:6)

Rabb is often translated as Lord. Unfortunately, when using
English, biblical Christian terminology perverts the original
meaning contained within the Arabic text. *Rabb* is that which is
responsible for what is below it. For example, *rabb al-bayt* is 'the
lord, owner, or the one who is responsible for the household',
implying that He knows what is in the household. *Rabubiyah*
(lordship) implies knowledge of what is below it. *Rabb* is essentially One who is responsible for bringing what is below it to its
full potential. Those who deny their Lord are in the punishment
of hell.

Jahannam (fire) has several meanings. The most common one
comes from the word *jahnim* meaning 'a bottomless pit'. In the
Qur'an it is described as the worst situation:

> Then therein (in *Jahannam*) he shall neither live
> nor die.
>
> (87:13)

It is a 'no man's land', in constant flux, a state undesirable to
man. We are programmed by our innate disposition *(fitrah)* to
want confirmation and firmness. We want to be free of the unknown. If we do dive into the unknown, it is only to experience
the joy of the unknown that lies at the end of the journey. *Jahnim*
means 'the pit'. It is that state in which nothing gels. One neither
lives nor dies. In the pit or fire, caught between life and death,
there is constant agitation which is the situation of the *kafir* (the
one who denies the truth). The *kuffar* (plural of *kafir*) cannot
accept the fact that there are still Muslims whom they have not
overcome. The war which the *kuffar* wage against the Muslims
is a human challenge, not a political conspiracy. Muslims are
not permitted to live within Islam by the *kuffar* because Islam
makes their consumerism, materialism and idolatry clear and
obvious.

Late in the last century, until about 1880, there existed many
Muslim enclaves, perhaps twenty, which extended from North
Africa to parts of China. The Muslims in these enclaves never
cared to know what was happening to the people in Europe
whom they regarded as barbarians. They assumed that if any
of them were any good they would come to them and embrace
Islam. They closed themselves up in their city-states, never looking outward. It was always the Europeans who were looking
across their borders into the Islamic East. Finally, the Europeans
penetrated the citadels of Islam by the practice of medicine. In
the West, an impressive medical science based upon cause and
effect was developed and this science, together with the European
system of education, was the bait that attracted the Muslims
and broke their trust in Allah and His religion. The western
medical practice was attractive, giving quick results. But look
at the medical situation now in the West: its cost is great and
its effect is minimal. It is based entirely on materialism. Man is
treated like a machine whose organs are cut out or replaced with
little thought.

Those who deny the state of loss in which the so-called modern civilization is in, are in *al-Jahannam* (the Fire), or versions of it, here and now.

> ...and evil is the resort.
>
> (67:6)

Ultimately, the deniers will be in the final *Jahannam* which is in non-time. Here within the brackets of time, they run from one satisfaction to another, consumers never satisfied because, quite naturally, the more the senses are fed, the more they demand. One's concern for the beautification of a room becomes a concern for an entire house; then the environment, the landscape, one's city, one's country. So we are ransacking the entire world for the sake of beauty. The consumers, the *kuffar*, flee to this world seeking their destiny. There is no time to reflect; it is not permitted. Even physical reflection is limited. Mirrors are put on the front door, permitting one moment of reflection as they dash out. Because of this situation, it is easy for gurus to fool them. The *kuffar* are easily cheated because they are cheating themselves. Every now and then you hear of a great spiritual movement. But these movements eventually collapse because they are not based on the fundamental principles which form the basis of Islam.

> When they shall be cast therein, they shall hear a loud moaning of it as it heaves.
>
> (67:7)

Fara means 'to boil over, froth at the mouth'. Businessmen may be seen foaming at the mouth if their business deals have not gone through.

> Almost bursting for fury. Whenever a group is cast into it, its keeper shall ask them: Did there not come to you a warner?
>
> (67:8)

Fawj is 'group', specifically, a battalion. Here we are given a parable of the next life, of *Jahannam* — the ultimate fire.

Whenever a group of energies is flung in to the fire, it meets its destiny according to the ultimate balance of action and reaction. Its keeper is the entity, the reality, the energy which keeps the state, the black hole, which is the *Jahannam*. *Khazana* is 'to store, to safeguard, to look after'. The keepers ask, 'Didn't you hear the warning?'

> They shall say: Yea! Indeed there came to us a
> warner, but we rejected (him) and said: Allah has
> not revealed anything; you are only in a great error.
> (67:9)

This is a clear declaration of *kufr*, the denial of the truth. As you know there are degrees of *kufr* and degrees of *shirk* (association with other than Allah), and the latter is included in the forms. Every *kafir* (denier) is a *mushrik* (one who associates with other than Allah). Any state that occurs to us which is not completely supported upon the platform of *"la ilaha illa 'llah Muhammadun rasulu'llah"* (there is no god but Allah and Muhammad is His messenger) clearly is an act of *kufr and shirk*. But we are optimists, we do not want to be reminded at all times of our faults, rather, we wish to be encouraged. The Prophet said, "Be optimistic about goodness and you shall find it." If we say:

> Allah has not revealed anything... .
> (67:9)

then we have denied that anything has descended upon us and that there is a possibility of ascent. To this human condition Allah says: "Surely man is at a loss." If we do not see a descent of guidance from the Creator to us, then there is nothing other than the *dunya*, the life of this world, and we are worse than animals because then we have become isolated from one another and selfish. Actually, we have become lower than the animals because while both the life of man and that of an animal consists of eating, sleeping, and fornicating, only the animal is content with his situation — man is not, he is troubled. We are already programmed not to be content with the hypothesis that,

> Allah has not revealed anything... .
> (67:9)

It is Allah's mercy upon us. We are already programmed in our innate disposition to call upon Allah, to want to know Allah, to be with Allah, and to not go any other way but the way of Allah.

> And they shall say: Had we but listened or pondered, we should not have been among the inmates of the burning fire.
>
> (67:10)

Often, we find in the Qur'an that *sam'*, the sense of hearing, occurs in man before *basr*, the sense of sight. One of the reasons why this is so is because biologically, genetically, man hears first before he sees. In the womb we only hear, we do not see. It is only later, after our birth, that we begin to see.

> So they shall acknowledge their sins, but far will be (forgiveness) from the inmates of the burning fire.
>
> (67:11)

Sahaqa in Arabic means 'to pulverize, to crush into the smallest possible state'. The situation in the next life will be such that they will be pulverized to almost nothingness and yet they will be something, *mashruq* (powder) — something which cannot be made smaller.

This *ayah* describes the state of being which has no reality, no possibility. It is a non-entity. The inmates of the Fire did not hear, nor did they use their reason concerning Allah's commands. Allah has created and has established his Command. It is up to us to bring into fruition the recognition of Allah's question to His slaves "Am I not your Lord?" Allah has done His part, we have to do the rest. The test which we must endure in this life causes us to examine whether or not we acknowledge Allah's part and the part that we must play in the events of this life. The people of the Fire did not examine the position of Allah and their own part while they had the opportunity.

> (As for) those who fear their Lord in secret, they shall surely have forgiveness and a great reward.
>
> (67:12)

So Allah,

> Blessed is He in Whose hand is the Kingdom... .
>   (67:4)

first gives us warning of chastisement for those who do not ponder the message that is sent to them. In this *ayah* Allah has given us the good news: the people of the Path "fear their Lord in secret." The Qur'an uses the word *al-ghayb* (the unseen, unknown), therefore, the rightly guided fear what may come to them because of what they have not seen. They trust that what Allah has revealed to them is true even though they have not yet come to know it. In other words, they accept what Allah has promised just as the scientist accepts any hypothesis or theory that is proven in the physical sciences. He first accepts a hypothesis, then tries to disprove it. If he cannot disprove it, it remains accepted as true. Here our assumption is the reality of the Unseen. As believers, we accept the fact that we have come from the unknown, are sustained by the unknown, and return back to the unknown. Our life journey's purpose is to come to know the unknown. To do this we start by seeking to understand what is in front of us. Allah's way is to take us through trials. Indeed, Allah says that He pulls many to the Garden on bleeding knees. Often, it is by passing through a time of trouble that we are made to turn towards the nature of reality. In these moments of difficulty we ask ourselves, 'Why am I unhappy? Why am I miserable?' The prophets were often found to be among people who were desperate. The drunkard finds drink to be a remedy for his incessant worrying. That is what that drug does — it stops you being the clobbered, down-trodden fellow of yesterday. Surely what he wants is forgetfulness of his yesterday so that he is freer to act in his tomorrow. We are the same, wanting to do our best for the sake of our future in the knowledge that whatever comes is the ultimate outcome according to the laws of the Creator. We seek to be in the here and now, inwardly totally drunk, outwardly totally sober. Inwardly, we want to be absolutely free, outwardly, absolutely constricted.

> And conceal your word or manifest it, surely He
> is Cognizant of what is in the hearts.
>   (67:13)

One of the meanings of *sharaha* is 'to bring near what appears
to be far'. *Tashrih* is 'dissection — looking at something closely,
to make something evident'. Allah says in a *Hadith Qudsi:*

> The heavens and earth do not contain Me but the
> heart of the mu'min (the believer) contains Me.

If the *sharh* (the elucidation) has occurred then we see the Mercy
of Allah everywhere, even when it hits us on the head time and
again. If a stone should fall on your head, it is the Mercy of
Allah reminding you that the law of gravity is a reality which,
if it were not so, would cause the world to fly this way and that
way in complete chaos. When some misfortune befalls us, usually
it is because we were unaware. We did not reflect or ask the
right advice. We went somewhere we were not supposed to be.

So, whether we keep what we do a secret or talk about it,
Allah knows. *Maqam al-ihsan* the upholding of goodness, is an
ongoing state in which we act, work, and live as though Allah
sees us at all times, with every breath. We act as though we are
constantly, perpetually under surveillance. Therefore, in the true
Islamic situation there are no privacies. For that reason, the
Qur'an admonishes the rough and aggressive people around the
Prophet not to scream at him nor shout at his door. They were
told to have some courtesy. Generally, those who are the true
followers of Muhammad are exposed, they have nothing to hide
and are available at all times. But without the right courtesy,
these men of service will be abused by those around them. They
will not be permitted the proper time to carry out their responsibilities to their families, and soon. If we are with Allah, He
will show us what is relevant to us at the relevant time. The
Prophet said: "Oh Allah, give me useful knowledge *('ilm an-
nafi'an)* ".

If we are truly in abandonment, in *iman* (faith, trust, belief),
Allah will show us what is relevant. The Prophet *'Isa* (Jesus)
said, "I came to a people who were desiring the Garden and
said, 'You will avoid what you fear.' I came to a people who
were worshipping for the sake of worship and I said 'You are
my people'." If we are true men of abandonment, we have nothing

to ask from Allah for we acknowledge that He is giving us what we need whereas we do not know what we need because we are separate from Him.

> And the last of their cry shall be: Praise be to Allah, the Lord of the worlds.
>
> (10:10)

"Praise be to Allah, the Lord of the worlds" is a statement of fact. When we say "In the Name of Allah, the Beneficent, the Merciful, Praise be to Allah," we mean that by Allah's creational laws, the praise belongs to Allah. *Al-hamd* is 'the glorification, the praise'. Whatever we may praise in creation, ultimately, we are praising not it but its Creator. It is the Decree of Allah that praise belongs to Allah. Actually, we are not bringing praise into being by our saying it. It is an absolute statement which existed before we were born, as we were born, as we die. *Al-hamdu lillah* is very different from *al-shukru lillah* (the thanks belongs to Allah). When *shukr* is proclaimed there is a separation between the one who is proclaiming his thankfulness and Allah. *Shukr* should not be said too often during the prayer because it is a statement of separation and *salat* is a statement of unification *(tawhid)*. *Shukr* implies the thanker and the thanked. It means that I recognize something that is bringing me contentment, whether it is knowledge, food or whatever. It is bringing me tranquillity so I say *'al-shukru lillah'*. *Al-hamdu lillah* is abstract. Allah says of Himself:

> Whatever is in the heavens and the earth declares the glory of Allah, and He is the Mighty, the Wise.
>
> (57:1)

It is a final statement.

11

The Witnesser and the Witnessed

As Muslims we inherit the belief that there is One Reality encompassing all existence both perceivable and imperceivable. We believe in One God — we believe in Allah. Therefore, praise belongs to the One and Only Reality. Whatever or whoever we may praise, we know that ultimately;

> All praise is due to Allah, the Lord of the Worlds.
>
> (1:1)

All praise goes back to Allah. By seeing this connection, we are on the path of unification with Allah. If we praise a good thing, we are ultimately praising the Creator of that thing.

So praise belongs to Allah. Those who see the one hand of Allah behind what appears to be diversity see the one interconnecting fibre and force. We experience life in this existence as a balance of opposites, whether it be ignorance and knowledge, health and illness, darkness and light, day and night, sleep and wakefulness, wealth and poverty, or life and death. What we conceive, or perceive, is necessarily one of a pair of opposites. Life cannot be experienced except as being composed of this balance. The melting pot of this existence is set up so that we interact, yet remain capable of discrimination, as the actors as well as the acted upon. We cannot avoid either of these two apparently opposite roles. At all times we are witnessing and being witnessed. At all times we are involved in a situation and yet have an awareness, a higher consciousness, of the situation.

This is the greatest puzzle and the source of the greatest gift of life for mankind — for the children of the Prophet Adam. If man perceives a dilemma or a situation which is not harmonious, it is because he has not seen what has brought about that situation. Looking back into the history of mankind, we find that man has been a seeker in whose primal nature there is programmed the desire to know whence he has come and whither he is going. From the time when the cell divided into multiplicity, we were programmed subgenetically with the desire to know the meaning of time, with the curiosity to know where we were before experiencing time and life, and where are we going after this experience ceases.

Some of us are more anxious about the experience of death than others. While some of us accept it simply as their inheritance, others are anxious to know and experience it here and now. The Prophet says: "Die before you die." The Prophet, being a most kind, generous and gentle being, did not mean that this life should be a slaughterhouse. What he meant was that one should experience the meaning of death in order to experience absolute purity of heart in this life. The Qur'an says:

> So when you are free, still toil. And make your
> Lord your exclusive objective.
>
> (94:7–8)

What is meant by 'free' is the emptiness which manifests in the mind when there is no thought, implying a life free from agitations. The reflection of this state is described in the Qur'an when Allah says:

> So that you may not grieve for what has escaped
> you, nor be exultant at what He has given you.
>
> (57:23)

This means that the situation most conducive to a noble life is that of being aware and alert to the here and now.

We are obviously the products of our past thoughts and actions interacting with the thoughts and actions of the people around us. The present state of affairs is the result of this interaction, and the future will be what we now make of it. According to the Qur'an and the Sunnah (the sayings and doings of the Prophet), man's condition as God's representative or *Khalifah* is to be the slave of the moment (*'abd al-waqt*). This means he should be completely present from one moment to the next moment. The slave of the moment is not an irresponsible person who cares little about tomorrow or about his past mistakes, rather, he is a man whose energies are totally available to him when he needs them. He is efficient because he is undisturbed either by the past or by the future, and therefore he is able to harness all his will to the present. When the *muezzin* calls the Muslims to prayer, he cries out, *"Hayya 'ala'l-falah"* (come to success). *Falah* is connected with the verbal root *falaha* whose meaning is to plough the earth, turn the earth, which, by extension, means 'to turn the heart' and therefore encompasses all the parts that one plays in life.

If there is any dilemma facing us in this life, whether it be how to improve our state or our quality of life as Muslims, our one underlying goal is to attain a state in this existence which will fully prepare us for the next experience about which we know nothing. One thing we know for certain: we will taste death. There is no escaping it. It is a statement of fact that we share with each other in the hope that we can reflect upon it and find our own personal meanings and conclusions.

The knowledges available to man are unchanging and of two types. One is technological, informational, transmittable from the common man to the common man. It is mechanistic knowledge concerned with outer technology such as how to use a dishwasher or how to drive a car. Although it may influence our mechanistic existence, it has no effect upon our emotional life. There is another type of knowledge, primal in nature, whose ultimate form is divine inspiration — the revealed knowledge, the knowledge of the prophets who were the interspace, the interlink, between the Ultimate Reality, the Knower of all things *(al-'Alim)* and the rest of mankind.

If I inherited a defect in my eye or in my finger, though my will may not be able to alter it, it could take me to a position in which the deformity had no significance. What is of ultimate significance is the will to know Reality, is the will to know Allah.

Why not discover the nature of reality now? We investigate the physical laws in order to bring about harmony in our environment. We want to understand causality; we want to know the physics and mathematics of the existentially relevant aspects of our lives. Why? We seek to control the temperature of the air in our homes so that the body is without agitation. Then we seek to have financial security so that we are not worried about how we are going to feed or clothe ourselves or our dependants tomorrow. Then what? If a person is confronted with the possibility of having guaranteed health for the next ten years and any of the homes he wants — one winter home, one summer home, and that he will have no need to worry about feeding or clothing himself and his family and still have some income left for the uncertainties of life, what is he going to do? Honestly, what is next?

It is an incontrovertible fact that man is a seeker whose seeking begins at a low physical level and extends to higher levels in order to reach a state of relative harmony and peace. From the beginning we are seekers of death because the ultimate peace is death. We are programmed with the desire to know whence we have come and whither we are going. And we are also equally conditioned to be somewhat scared of this awesome experience called death, for we try to postpone it, knowing all the time that every day we are closer to it. Yet even though we are rational beings we prefer to do nothing but drift on towards the inevitable, using different excuses to cover up the fact that we have not the courage to confront this incredible unknown.

Besides having to face an awesome unknown, we perceive something within us which says that death is very unfair. After years of having squandered thousands of tons of consumables in the form of food, air, fuel or whatever, and after having gained in experience and wisdom, we are suddenly deposited, at best, under six feet of dust. It seems pretty unfair, as though something is nòt right. It seems unjust. The Qur'an says:

> And We did them no injustice, but they were unjust
> to themselves.

> (16:118)

We do to ourselves an injustice by not utilizing our diminishing capital which is the time in which we are alive. Although everything else is replaceable, time can neither be replaced nor reversed. We will experience the non-time zone which is the definition of the next life, but as for this present experience, it is sustained by a dynamic factor called time which is non-directional. Allah, on the other hand, is not bounded by time. He is beyond time — He is the First and the Last so He encompasses time; therefore as Muslims we say:

> Surely we are Allah's and to Him we shall surely
> return.
>
> (2:156)

If that is the case then why are we so concerned?

"Actions are determined by intentions and to each (individual)
is his intention." If our intention is to attain knowledge and
apply it in our lives, then we are intending to unify the inner
and the outer. Islam is the path of unification *(tawhid)*, the path
of unifying the inner and the outer, the seen and the unseen. A
Muslim has to believe in the unseen, the next life and what are
called the angels. Angels can be imagined as being specifically
defined bundles of energy. Our experiential physics has reached
but the tip of the iceberg. The whole physical reality is sustained
and supported by a much subtler reality which science has just
begun to perceive.

As rational human beings, we can accept that there is an
underpinning to creation that is so subtle that we cannot know
it in its specifics. Yet we can accept that there is an order to
which the entities called angels belong. Indeed we have to accept
these facts as Muslims, we have no option. We have to accept
the path of Islam. We have to accept The Qur'an. We have to
accept the *sunnah* of the blessed Prophet.

Muslims born into Muslim families are suffering from the
dilemma of having inherited the Islamic model. Fortunately, of
course, Islam is uninheritable; on the contrary, it has to be
earned. Throughout the ages Muslim communities have experienced cycles of revival and decline. It is in the nature of reality
that whenever Islamic culture and civilization reaches its zenith,
its people begin to take it for granted, and lead this to its dilution.
The people no longer recognize the boundaries clearly and they
begin to transgress. Worship *('ibadah)* is the inner technology of
Islam, and when this is strong and its people are true slaves of
Allah *('ibad)*, then the outer technology of Islam surrounds them
in safety. Architecture and the forms of art are also peripheral
manifestations of an inner reality. Soon the wealth that living
according to Islam brings can lead to luxury which, as you know

from descriptions in the Qur'an, leads to the destruction of a people. The Qur'an says:

> And when we wish to destroy a town, We send Our commandment to the people of it who lead easy lives, but they transgress therein; thus the word proves true against it, so We destroy it with utter destruction.
>
> (17:16)

It is inevitable that there will be corruption as a result of decadence. We must determine what is necessary to attain our first priority, relative tranquillity. If our bodies are not relatively healthy, our nature is compelled to rectify that problem before all others. The body should be reasonably intact, the environment reasonably healthy. Then we need some clothing and food. Beyond that there are grey areas in terms of needs. Those who are pursuing the *dunya* or worldly existence will never stop seeking the things of this world. Ask a businessman what is enough? Whereas thirty years ago it would have been considered an insult to call someone aggressive, ambitious and competitive, today, especially in the business world, it would be taken as a compliment and a sign of the highest worth. When a bank advertises itself as 'aggressive', it means that it will callously forsake you when you need it most.

When Queen Isabella of Spain was on the Muslim borders of Andalusia, waiting to attack, she sent her spy into the city to the bazaar. He bought candles from a shop. He wanted to buy more, but the shop owner told him: "I have sold enough for today, please buy from my neighbour." The spy said, "No, I want to buy your candles, they seem to be better." He said, "No they are not better. I cannot sell you any more. It is now my neighbour's turn." When the spy returned, he told Isabella: "These people cannot be defeated, they are too powerful." Then, later in time, when decadence had set in, the spy came back to the same shop. This time the shop owner tells him, "I have the best goods in the bazaar. I have the best prices, the best quality." Immediately, the spy returns saying, "Now is the time to attack."

In the *sunnah* of the Prophet Muhammad, it is very clear: you are not to recommend your goods over the goods of others. Among true Muslims there are very subtle, but clear courtesies. When the Muslims lived as members of a strong and united community *(ummah)*, the non-Muslims around them were curious to know why the Muslims were so self-contained and content; why their culture was so superior.

Then the Europeans came into the Muslim citadels riding on the banners of service, basically health and education. They dominated the Muslim people through their possession of certain advanced techniques within the mechanistic side of health. These people were, and still are, mechanistic and materialistic, and this is partly because of their environment. One cannot live in a cold climate without being materialistic. It is not possible to live in the north of England and not be constantly concerned about sufficient fuel for the winter.

In the warmer climates, the reverse is true. It is a burden to have too many clothes. As a young man I came to live in a village at the southern tip of India where the staple diet was fish. The people had been living in great harmony. The village was composed of Muslims and Christians, yet as long as they could remember there had been no problems or strife among them. These people literally lived the whole year with only two loincloths. They had no need of anything more than that because the climate was so benign.

At the moment throughout the so-called Muslim countries, Muslims share the same desire for Islam. They know that therein lies their salvation, but they do not know how to bring it into reality. Most Muslims live under Muslim governments of varying degrees of hypocrisy. The Prophet said that a good intention was enough. But, although we may be redeemed by the purity of our hearts, the recipient of our actions may still have reason to complain. For example, I have the intention of painting a house using the best materials and best techniques, but out of a lack of knowledge about painting, I make a terrible mess. I may feel good that I have done my best, yet the owner of the house will have received nothing but a headache.

Our goal is to harmonize our intentions with the outcome, the inner with the outer. We must be men of *tawhid* (unification), otherwise, we are not in Islam. We have to unify the intention with the outer result. The Muslim wants success. We should remember the phrase in the call to prayer: *"hayya 'ala'l-falah"* (come to success). We need to leave this world both having done our best and seen its results. If we fail to use the Qur'an as a manual for correct and effective action, then we have missed its meaning. Decadence and corruption spreads because the people are not getting inner nourishment. If they cannot get this nourishment, quite naturally they pursue the path towards outer fulfilment.

If you are not able to see the Creator's handywork at every corner. If you are unable to take delight in a simple life. If you are unable to see the magnificence of this creation. If you are not drunk with the incredible gift of life. If you are not prepared to be intoxicated simply because you have been given the gift of being able to see though only for a brief moment. If you have not been trained in these ways you will be trained to make a quicker buck on the side. What else can you do?

If you have energy, an intellect, and time on your hands Shaytan will divert you. The Prophet said, "Everyone has a shaytan. But I have been given the gift of knowing my shaytan, and therefore he is under my control." Shaytan is present to keep us alert and make us aware of our potential to make mistakes. Shaytan can teach us the boundaries of proper action and thought.

The Qur'an says:

> I swear by time, Most surely man is in loss.
>
> (103:1–2)

and:

> Nay, most of them do not understand.
>
> (29:63)
> And most of them do not hear, and most of them
And n do not see.
>
> (11.20)

If man is at a loss at the physical, existential or basic state, this enables him to rise upward. From this platform he is powered to take off through the motive of discontent. No matter where we look there is discontent. If we were content it would be a sign that something was wrong. How can we be content with ourselves when there is always something more that we can do? If we turn towards materialism we find that we can never get enough; and if we turn towards spiritualism we find ourselves increasingly concerned about the purity of our intentions and ever seeking to leave the results to Allah and living the moment. By purifying our intentions and leaving the outcome to Allah, we will encounter what is best for us, what is guaranteed by Allah. We must remember that this life is Allah's arena, Allah's creation and Allah's plot.

If we enslave ourselves to this truth, we will cease to be a slave to any other reality or being. We will then be fearless of everything other than Allah. We will be courageous and willing to give up this life at any moment. Islam gives us this willingness because it teaches us that our life begins after death. And if, in this life, we have invested for the next, there is no need to fear death and what follows. It is un-Islamic to fear death and yet we find that, in the so-called Muslim societies, people are afraid of talking about it. The Prophet said, "This world is the believer's prison and the unbeliever's garden." It is a prison for the believer because he already contains within him the meaning of the cosmos, therefore his body confines him and is a nuisance.

"Beware of the believer's insight," said the blessed Prophet. The man of true faith has the gift of insight. By means of this gift he can quickly assess the extent of the illness of a person or society. So I share with you the news that we are sick. But in this knowledge is half of the cure.

Once we accept the fact of our illness, we will find a way to the cure. One of the main causes is our lack of discrimination. We are in a state of unclarity, whereas Islam demands clarity. The Prophet said, "There are things that are correct and things that are wrong, take what is correct and avoid what is incorrect." Between these two there are many shades. We tend to allow our actions to fall within this grey, unclear area, because we have not as yet developed and applied the science of the *nafs* (the self).

Islam spread through the efforts of the Sufis. These were men of inner knowledge who knew how to cure the self. Today we often find, even in great institutions of knowledge, that something is lacking. Usually there is a lot of outer knowledge — knowledge of the Qur'an, the *Sunnah*, the *Shari'ah* and the *Sirah* (the life of the Prophet), but somehow these knowledges are not directly applied. The knowledge (*'ilm*) and the action (*'amal*) have not become one. And as we all know, little knowledge applied is far better than a lot of knowledge not applied. The reason why we are not able to apply our knowledge is because our *nafs* (the self) has been allowed to get in the way. We have not been watching our *nafs* nor have we been aware of its interference between our knowledge and our action. Actually, as a result of the confused state of our self, we will intend one thing but our actions will result in something else. This is, of course, contrary to *tawhid*, the path of unification which is Islam. So something is wrong; not with Islam but with how we apply our knowledge. I, the self, has destroyed the intended project: some of me wanted one thing, another part of me wanted another, therefore, I have not been clear. That which is in us, the confusion, must become manifest. There is a tradition that the Prophet said: "Tell me where a person lives and what he eats and I can tell you who he is." You cannot be a man of simplicity, clarity, purity, and live in confusion. Such a thing is impossible. If you want Allah, you will get Allah. Allah says in the words of a *hadith qudsi:*

> If you take one step towards Me, I will take ten
> steps towards you.

Like most of you here, I was given Islam as a gift by my parents and by the blessed people of Karbala where I grew up. During the years that I have lived there I never heard of a theft. There were no policemen, nor hospitals. Most of my ancestors, including my grand-mother, died in their nineties, even in their hundreds. I did not dare misbehave in the street for fear that someone would grab me and bring me home and say, 'Look! Your son was being disorderly.' There was no disorderliness. People knew each other. There was harmony. There was not much wealth, but all the food was fresh. In the centre of my house was an enormous kitchen in the middle of which was a big fire. Usually half a dozen elderly women would be around it having a good time, enjoying their lives there. Although they were servants, they were not considered socially inferior, rather they were considered more important than even my own mother.

Now that whole way of life has been destroyed. Today Karbala is a city of villas, cars, banks, and worries about higher interest rates. Now there are hospitals, ulcers, and imported drugs. What have we done with our traditional sciences? For example, Islamic medicine was an outer manifestation of an inner reality of Islam. The doctors in Islam *(hukama)* were servants of Allah. They would pray in the morning for Allah to send them someone whom they could help on the physical level so that eventually they could help him on the spiritual level. This was the true essence of medicine. Thus, medicine and spiritual teaching were working hand in hand. They did not separate physical well-being from inner well-being. Being Muslims, we have access to a great and powerful body of knowledge, in medicine as well as in other sciences. The Prophet said: "There is a lump in a man's chest; if it is well, everything is well, and if it is not well, then nothing is well; and it is called the heart." The root of the Arabic word, as you all know, is *qalb* and the verb is *qalaba, yaqlibu* (to turn). That means it is fresh, it is not stuck, it is not connected with one thing, it is connected with the One and only One. It turns. When people used to come to the Prophet and told him that a certain thing had happened, that a certain person had broken something, he would ask: "Did it happen?" They would say: "Yes." He would say: "(Glory be to Allah) it happened, what can we do? It is done, it is the will of Allah." This means: we were negligent. The will of Allah manifested in the form of the laws of gravity, the thing fell. The will of Allah manifests in a perfect, understandable, logical sense. Allah does not work in an illogical way. When we call something a miracle, it is because we are ignorant about the scenes that brought it about. We call something lucky because we do not understand all the physical and other forces that brought it about. It is a confession of our ignorance that is all and we will remain ignorant no matter how much we know. There is bound to be a certain measure of ignorance.

The situation we are in is fully understandable and it is our own doing. If we complain, it is out of ignorance. We have given priority to outer physical knowledge as opposed to inner knowledge. We have sought to acquire outer rather than inner technology. We have lost touch with our own hearts. If, in my heart, I intend to be nasty to my wife, bringing her flowers will be no use. The lie will be apparent even to the children. We cannot lie, the liar lies to himself. The cheater cheats himself. Allah says in the Qur'an:

> If you are good to one person you are good to all
> creation, if you are bad to one person you are bad
> to all creation.
>
> (17:7)

The meaning of this is that we are all from one self. The believers are brothers. If we believe that, and we truly come to know it, then we see everyone as our brother. Maybe some of them are asleep, but potentially they are our brothers.

> He brings forth the living from the dead and brings
> forth the dead from the living, and gives life to the
> earth after its death, and thus shall you be brought
> forth.
>
> (30:19)

Allah says, how do you know what will happen to him tomorow? He may be far more fully awake than you and I. We have no right to turn our faces and be arrogant simply because at that stage we are in a better state of knowledge, or health, or wealth or whatever. How do we know?

The Prophet says: "You are not a Muslim if you greet a poor man differently than a wealthy man." Do we greet our kings and presidents the same way as we greet the beggar at the door of Sayyid 'Ali Hujwiri? We have to be honest, we have to be aware of what we are doing and what state we are in. Then we should be able to unify the inner with the outer. What is missing, to a great extent, is the knowledge of the *nafs* (self). This is a much neglected science.

As I mentioned earlier, those who were carrying the banner

of Islam were generally masters of the self. They were the people whom you would call Sufis or men of gnosis *('irfan)* and real knowledge *('ilm)*; they were firmly established or thoroughly versed in their knowledge of Islam. The Qur'an says:

> Say! Are the blind and the seeing one alike? Do
> you not then reflect?
>
> (6:50)

The living of Islam requires perception and reflection, the application of the science of the self. We must know what is in ourselves: what is our intention? Why are we here? If I am here in front of you only for my personal benefit, then I have failed myself and everyone else. But my reason for being here is to share what little I know, as a result of the great opportunities with which Allah has blessed me. With this aim in mind, I can avoid adding more arrogance and vanity to myself. Then my service could be considered as *fi sabili'llah* (in the way of Allah).

> We desire from you neither reward nor thanks.
>
> (76:9)

Only if we are acting completely in the way of Allah are we saved from disappointment. It is a scientific way of overcoming all so-called psychological problems. Unless our hearts are contained and content with the beauty and the majesty of the manifestations of the Creator, materialism will prevail, bringing with it all of its ills. You cannot prevent people from being greedy because we are born greedy; but essentially we are greedy for the knowledge of Allah. If we are not put on that path, we will be greedy for that which is physical. Today, instead of mosques and temples, people attend halls of worship called banks which resemble the old Gothic cathedrals. If you go to Europe or America you will see what I am talking about. The bank has a huge high ceiling; it is as if one has entered into a cathedral. Most people think that money is the key to freedom. They do not realize that they are the slaves of the bank manager. When the bank manager phones, the hand sweats.

What I would like to share with you is good news and bad

news at the same time. They manifest together because this life hinges on opposites. The good news is that we have the way which is the Qur'an. The Qur'an is in our hearts, but we have to dig it out. It is under the debris of accumulated habits, inattentiveness, insensitivity and ignorance. Dispel the darkness of ignorance and the light of knowledge which was already there will shine. This is nothing new. The light of the knowledge of Reality is innate. The practice of *salat* (prayer) five times a day is part of the process which polishes the heart; provided, of course it is a true *salat*, which has within it the song of *al-hamdu lillah* (glory be to Allah), provided it is genuinely from your heart. In the *Fatiha* which is repeated so often in the prayer, we say *Bismillahi Rahmani Rahim* (In the Name of Allah, the Compassionate, the Merciful). *Al-hamdu lillahi Rabbil-'alamin* (Glory be to Allah, the Lord of the Worlds). *Ar-Rahmani-Rahim* (The Beneficent, the Merciful). This is His description. He is *Al-Rahman*, the Merciful for all the world and *Al-Rahim*, the Compassionate for individuals. Then Allah says of Himself, *Maliki Yawm al-Din* (Owner of the Day of Reckoning). What is the Day of Reckoning? The Qur'an describes it as:

> The day in which no soul shall be of the least avail
> to another; and the command on that day shall be
> entirely Allah's.
>
> (82:19)

Why don't we realize that the Day of Reckoning is occurring each day? There will be the big one, the eternal one, the cosmic one, but there is also the daily *yawm al-din* in which I am taken to account. Each day I should see my balance sheet. As a businessman I am prudent to do that regularly. Why delay looking at the balance sheet of my life until the moment of my death? Why not keep the moment of death in front of me at every moment? Then I will treasure life and it will become real.

This is the path of Islam. If the prayers are performed with sincerity, if ablutions *(wudu)* are done five times a day, we are replenished, reborn. These are the provisions of the wayfarers as they travel on their short journey through life. How many years have gone by? And how many moments within those years

have we really been aware? What are we doing and why are we
doing it? The Qur'an says:

> Now surely by Allah's remembrance are the hearts
> set at rest.
>
> (13:28)

The good news is that we have the way, the power of discrimination, which is the Qur'an; we have the *sunnah* (the sayings and
doings of the Prophet). If we have had the blessedness of being
born in Islam, we must ask ourselves whether we have earned
what we have inherited.

The bad news is that in the East we have tarnished our situation to such an extent that there is mass confusion. For that
reason, it is much easier to have discrimination in a non-Muslim
land where everything is forbidden *(haram)*. We are surrounded
by enemy territory in the sense that we are surrounded by ignorance. The ignorant are enemies to themselves though they do
not know it; they have not yet received the good news. Whilst
it is easier for us in the West, we have to lower our eyes wherever
we walk: whatever we see is likely to harm us. We have to be
careful what we touch, where we eat. There will be no change
if we do not change, and the sooner we begin the better. The
signs are that the end of time is almost here. Most of the signs
mentioned in the hadiths indicate that Imam Mahdi may be
here at any time. So we take heed and do our best to prepare
ourselves for the time when the earth will be governed justly. If
each one of us tries to set an example for his own sake, then we
have done it for Allah's sake.

Allah's light, the knowledge of Allah, will prevail everywhere.
This knowledge is the knowledge of the laws of Allah which are
clear if we want to know them. The clarity of those laws will
become absolute if we enter into Islam with complete abandonment as upright noble beings. Total submission contains within
it the trust and belief that, even if we do not know now, we will
come to know: the root of knowledge which is within us will
awaken.

12

The Spiritual Nature of Man

Whether we believe in any religion, or in God, or in any other value system, there are certain aspects of life that concern us all. These aspects are so fundamental that they do not depend upon one's background, heritage, or belief. The best way of approaching this subject is to first consider the nature of man's spirit. In this way one can avoid becoming bogged down in linguistic and philosophical definitions.

Spirit, in the English language, may mean essence, cause, or nature. If we try to look into our essence, where does it take us to? What is this thing within every other human being that guides us or misguides us? What is it that drives us to do anything? What is it that causes us to want something or not want something else? What is it that makes us tick? What creates desires in us and what satisfies these desires? What do we feel or experience when a desire is satisfied? Why are we constantly searching for satisfaction, never satisfied? What is the nature of man that makes him constantly dissatisfied?

These things are beyond creed, nationality, religion or systems of belief. They are basic. The Arabic term is *fitri* (primal). This is our nature: we are always looking for something else. Whenever one obtains satisfaction or tranquillity from that which one was seeking, the mind by its nature moves to something else. This process does not cease. One is tired and wants to sleep; one has slept long enough and thus wants to get up. One is hungry and wants food; after filling the stomach, one wants to stop eating. One wants to be sheltered from environmental pressures, to control the ecological situation. As soon as a modicum of control is attained, one wants to know what to do within the system.

Let us examine libraries for example. Once these enormous places are built, those responsible must worry about how they are going to fill the building with books. What, one wonders, is the value of all these books? We now have more information and less knowledge. In this age we have such an accumulation of facts, which can be useful, but no method of knowledge to utilize those facts so that we can attain the satisfaction that we are all seeking.

So if we look at the nature of man's spirit, what drives us on at all times, wherever we are, in whatever environment, is this need to achieve desires that are never constant. The desires of a child change all the time and so do the desires of an adult. The higher we move biologically or intellectually, the subtler our desires become. At a lower basic level, we are very physical; we want to be clothed and fed in order to be in a reasonable balance, without agitation. We want to have enough food in order not to be disturbed, because biologically the stomach signals until a pang of pain disturbs us. Equally we want to avoid that which impinges on us from the outside and is not conducive to a state of tranquillity, therefore, we close the door so that we are not disturbed, to make sure that we have reasonable protection from the sound and noise. Thus, at all times, whatever we perceive, conceive, desire, anything that motivates us from within or without fits into this scheme.

Look into this deeply, contemplate upon it and you will find that what drives us, what makes us act or think, is basically a state of dynamism seeking equilibrium, seeking a position of neutrality. It is a very strange affair. At all times the spirit of man is guided, driven and propelled by the pursuit of peace. Yet, at the same time, we are the creators of that agitation. It is incredible if we really reflect upon it.

What drives man is an ongoing quest, sometimes rational, sometimes not, sometimes emotional, sometimes intellectual. There is a natural, primal hierarchy which fluctuates up or down, generally moving from the physical towards the subtle. The equilibrium that a child seeks is physical. The equilibrium sought by those who have satisfied their basic needs is intellectual. We try to keep our bodies in a reasonable state of equilibrium because, unless we have done this, we cannot progress further.

After the bodily level comes the mental level. Our mind has to be at rest. If my mind is agitated about something or some situation, then this irritation will disrupt my equilibrium, sapping the strength of my mental energy.

We are here discusssing aspects of knowledge that go beyond

quantification and formulation. Formulas can be applied to them if one wishes and those formulas will change from system to system. But the fundamental issue remains the same: if the physical, mental and intellectual levels are disturbed, equilibrium and balance are not possible. That to which our spirit drives us one may describe it loosely by the term happiness — cannot be achieved. If we wish to express this as a mathematical equation, we may say that happiness equals desires satisfied over desires unsatisfied. Thus, if one has one hundred desires and fifty are satisfied, happiness is fifty percent achieved. So, mentally we also seek to be at ease, to avoid any issue that disturbs the mind. Mental expectations and attachments that are not met will cause disappointment which is a state of imbalance; and that is not desirable. We do not want to be disappointed, we want to be appointed.

Notice how people who are wealthy and do not wish to be disturbed place layers of secretaries as barriers between themselves and the outside world. Think of Howard Hughes: he died in a corner from malnutrition. We want peace, there is no way out of it. Those who are exposed to any spiritual system know that peace is a high attribute. Those who are Muslims know that peace is from *as-Salam*, one of the attributes of Allah, glory be to Him. We all want peace yet are constantly in dynamic agitation at all these levels — the physical, the mental and the intellectual. Those who seek knowledge do so because they have discovered within themselves an aspect referred to as ignorance and this is disquieting. That is why so many people move across from one corridor of an ivory tower to another saying, 'Well, the intellectual atmosphere of this college or school was not conducive.' This can often mean also that there was a nasty head of department. Man's agitations and troubles are everywhere. It makes no difference whether one is in the academic world, the business world, or the political world. Everyone is subjected to the same types of experience, and this is a proof, in fact, of the All-Encompassing Merciful One. Even the sanitation engineers and janitors feel jealousies. Be assured that there is a hierarchy among the bathroom cleaners.

Man's desire to avert disturbance and find equilibrium causes him to form alliances with people of the same orientation: "Birds of a feather flock together." It is natural and unavoidable. We ourselves are a proof of this basic cybernetic process. We do not want to be jolted out of our system, thus we find people of the same belief, lifestyle, or creed banding together.

The process of unification, in this case unifying desires with what will neutralize them, is a selective process. The child, as he starts crawling, tries to assimilate everything he encounters in order to unify with his environment. He picks up things and puts them in his mouth because this is the first and primary organ of unification — mouth to breast. Suddenly the child's mouth is frothing: he is spitting the thing out because it is not in unison with his system. If systems, whether they be psychological, social, ecological or mechanical, do not adapt, then they self-destruct. If a happy person sees someone else who is unhappy and informs him of his happiness, this is perceived as a challenge. The result is conflict, either overt or covert. This is why we see political systems continuously being overturned.

We have spoken about a simple proportional equation relating to happiness. Can that formula be equal to one? The number of desires satisfied equal to the number of desires? As we know, as soon as a situation is satisfied and brought into equilibrium, something else goes wrong. There is an old saying: "As soon as you plug it here, it bursts from there." We are caught in a non-stoppable dynamic situation. And yet, at all times we wish it would stop. If a situation is incongruous, we want it to cease. If it is agreeable, we want to stop it in time so that it will continue. This is why we take photographs, to remind ourselves of the state we were in when we saw our child smiling, or when we won the football game. The trophy is placed on the mantlepiece to remind oneself of the moments of achievement, the experience of tranquillity.

Returning to the point, we will never be able to avoid having desires, nor will we be able to achieve all our desires. So it seems, in a sense, a losing battle. But is the nature of reality so cruel? How can God, if we believe in Him, do this to us? How can we all be seeking happiness knowing full well that, by our own definition, it is unattainable? There is a basic incongruity in this situation. Here we are wanting to fixate things and we can only do it on Kodak film. This is not possible. Here we are desirous of unending peace and we cannot attain it even for a few seconds?

Try and attain total peace for five seconds. Try and sit completely and utterly tranquil with not a single thought in the mind. One may be aware of peace, silence, or tranquillity, but this is not what we are talking about. We are talking about pure consciousness that admits no awareness of itself; that is total, absolute peace. One may be aware of something nice, that is very tranquil, but that is agitation. One may also be aware of awareness, and also aware of the awareness of one's awareness. Two mirrors opposite each other illustrate well this condition. But can one be purely, simply, totally just awareness itself? Pure awareness.

Where do we go from here? Let us add another dimension. We will look at the same thing from another angle: our desire for complete peace is actually a desire for permanency, for foreverness. We want non-time. We are all dying, and yet we want to know the meaning of eternity. We do not want to die even though our lives may be miserable, even though we can never achieve our desires. Nobody in his right mind says 'I want to die', because we do not know the nature of what happens after the body is recycled. We have not had direct access to it. How do you resolve this problem? It is a dilemma similar to the so-called quest for happiness. At every moment we approach nearer to that unknown state after death, and whatever is unknown to us is our enemy. This is the nature of man. It is in our nature to seek knowledge for we do not like what is unknown. But information is not knowledge. And information without a unifying system brings about greater confusion, because there are so many extraneous facts. caught in this unending dichotomy, on the one hand wanting tranquillity, peace, satisfaction, and happiness, on the other hand knowing it is impossible, is there no way out? As soon as the thermostat is adjusted, the weather changes. It is not possible to fix it, and yet we are seeking a fixed, unchanging reality. In short, man is by nature a seeker who seeks a reality with the following attributes: it is unchanging, eternal, absolute, beyond time, the One who contains time, the

All-Merciful, the All-Generous. We all share the desire for these
fundamental attributes.

We all want wisdom because wisdom is knowledge acquired
through experience which may be applied again in the future,
so that if the same situation is repeated, we are able to avoid
unhappiness and agitation. Our agitations, incidentally, are all
due to the fact that we do not know the cause and effect of a
situation when it happens. Even in the case of a situation which
we find disagreeable, once it is explained to us how it occurred,
we will find much of the problem has dissipated. This is one of
the meanings of

> Surely with difficulty is ease.
> With difficulty is surely ease.
>
> (94:5–6)

There is a double ease with every difficulty. The first ease is that
the difficulty will eventually be removed. The other ease is to
know how the difficulty arose, for that knowledge in itself is a
relief. This means we are slaves of knowledge, we are slaves of
al-'Alim (the All-Knower). Only the foolish person says, 'Don't
tell me, don't give me bad news,' for the news will come whether
one sticks one's fingers in one's ears or closes one's eyes. Ultimately, the roof will come down. There is no hiding place.

> Man will say on that day: whither to fly to?
>
> (5:10)

As I have said, we are trapped because the spirit, the
mechanism that drives all of us, is the same — we all want to
avoid whatever is disquieting and the desires that must be neutralized to achieve this state change all the time. We are programmed sub-genetically to be caught in this dilemma and each one
must sort it out in his own way. There are as many ways to that
knowledge as there are human beings.

The knowledge process which illuminates this dilemma is what
we call self-knowledge. This fundamental fibre is what we can
define as true knowledge, because it does not change with time.
From the rise of the Adamic consciousness this fibre was present.

The Adamic consciousness was a unified consciousness until there was a need for differentiation, until the voice of dissent was heard, the voice of what is termed Shaytan (satan), from the Arabic verb *shatana* which means 'to be far away'. In other words, Shaytan refers to that which is out of line with the unified field of consciousness. From that moment differentiation was born, because prior to that Adam had not heard anything but truth. Suddenly, he heard something which he also thought to be the truth, for he was used to hearing nothing but the truth. In order for discrimination to occur, this rise of apparent two-ness is necessary. We should be able to observe ourselves and our lives, so that we may see how we are torn between the two and rooted in the One.

Ibn 'Arabi says that the entire creation is balanced between the two opposites of renunciation and appreciation — renouncing what we do not desire and appreciating what one values. We are caught and there is no way out. The essential nature of humanity has been and will always remain unchanged, regardless of a person's culture, nationality, or belief system.

The only possible resolution to this conflict is recognition of the dilemma and submission to it. This leads to sublimation, that is to say, to a process of spiritual transformation or refinement. We have explored the theme of recognition and seen the self from the standpoint of its motivation. From this frame of reference we can understand it in any of its manifestations. By seeing the reality of the self, we must then fully submit to the condition, dissolving into it, submitting to it with no expectations. We must allow that inner urge which has its foundation in non-time to push us higher and higher towards divine knowledge, towards divine awakening. We must use the divine law and the prophetic path to guide us, for only in this way can the proper balance between renunciation and appreciation be maintained.

We are aspiring towards the higher attributes of the self which are basically divine attributes. Thus, we may say that the essential nature of humanity is divine, yet it is mostly the lower nature which we see exhibited in our lives. The Qur'an clearly states the condition of this lower aspect of the self saying:

> Or do you think that most of them hear or under-
> stand? They are nothing but as cattle; nay they
> are straying farther off from the path.
>
> (25:44)

The rest of this condition is the desire. We all have basic desires that are very selfish and subjective, aimed at our own comfort and well-being. If we are given the opportunity to move on, our desires could be to share with others, with neighbours, with society, with mankind. Thus, this unavoidable condition of having desires is transformed higher and higher. If from the beginning we could make our desires for humanity, we could avoid our present troubles. What if the aim of our desire is to share knowledge, or to please Allah, this will mean that our desire will be to know the laws that govern this existence so we never transgress them. We cannot avoid desire, nor do we want to avoid it, otherwise we will be cabbages or artificial hermits. We cannot avoid it because the source and ultimate aim of desire is divine.

There was a man from a very wealthy family in England, from the Midlands. He really had renounced the world. For seven years he lived on almost ten pounds a year. There was such wonderful expression of freedom on his face and one could see that the man was free — except every Wednesday. Every Wednesday he would go to the local post office and collect a box of chocolates that some of his friends used to send from Switzerland. He would say: "I do not care for anything in the world but these chocolates. Everything is now concentrated in these chocolates." All his desires had concentrated on one object. Since we cannot be desireless, let us move our desires higher and higher. Ultimately we may reach an Entity about which we cannot speak, about which all what we can say is, "There is no god but God."

This method cannot just be studied, it has to be lived. Study without practice is yet another unworkable duality. As I have said, the only way out of our predicament is to submit totally to that Reality which encompasses all realities, both relative and subjective. We have to dissolve into it, submitting to it with no expectations. From this unified state another process emerges, another awakening begins to occur, which will offer us the means of being secure in this life. I am here referring to the *shari'ah*, the corpus of divine law which provides us with a mechanism for established equilibrium and progress.

13

The Path of Unity

A man who was pretending to be a Sufi came to Imam Ja'far as-Sadiq and asked the Imam, "Why are you dressed so beautifully, when your ancestors dressed in patched robes?" He replied, "I am not wearing anything that cannot be found in the bazaar at Medina." At that time, during the time of Mu'awiyyah, Medina was full of opulence and extremely decadent. Imam Ja'far as-Sadiq said to the man, "Go to the bazaar, and see if these robes are commonly available. Wealth has poured in from everywhere; everybody can afford them." The man did so, and found that in fact the abundance of wealth had produced an economic situation that made the robes commonly available and easily affordable. He returned to the Imam who explained, "I want to be like everyone else; I don't want to be different. I am dressing this way for you people. If I had my choice I would be dressed in what I am wearing underneath." He then showed him a coarse, patched robe that he was wearing underneath.

This story exemplifies the meaning of *dunya*. The true meaning of *dunya* is attachment to worldly existence in any form. There is nothing wrong with a beautiful car, but who owns whom?

We must come to understand the meanings of the self and how these meanings interconnect with the practice and courtesies of Islam. For example, let us consider anger, is it good or bad.?

It is both good and bad. If one is angry and indignant against evil, it is the right thing. If one is angry emotionally or because of one's *nafs* (self), it is terrible. One must be patient to see how correct anger may be shown in the way of Allah. Sometimes anger against evil should not be expressed. One should run away, let it subside, because one is in the wrong place at the wrong time. Anger is a great power. Channelled properly it is of benefit, like a river that is harnessed to irrigate fields. What are hopes and expectations? What is haughtiness? What is oppression? What is lust? Is it good or bad, and how is it channelled? What is the meaning of companionship and brotherhood? What is the

meaning of greeting? What are the courtesies of sitting and walking? There is much in Islam even about the courtesies of sneezing.
What is the meaning and courtesy of visiting each other, of giving
gifts to each other? What are the virtues of sickness? Much has
been written in our traditions about this subject. What is the
meaning of grief? How does it come about? Why is one occasionally depressed for no reason? We could go on and on.

What are the sicknesses of the self, and how can we cure them?
What is the meaning of *'aql*, the faculty of reasoning? What is
the heart, *al-qalb*, which should continuously turn? What is forgiveness? What is repentence? What is the meaning of divine
law? What is the meaning of *fiqh*, jurisprudence? What is the
meaning of ritual purity and of prayer? What is the meaning of
almsgiving? What is the meaning of the yearly payment of 2½%
of one's earnings after expenses in the way of Allah? What is the
meaning of pilgrimage to Mecca? What is the meaning of struggle
in way of Allah? When the Muslims returned from battle, the
Prophet told them, "Now you have come back from the lesser
battle; it is time for you to start the greater battle, the struggle
with the self in the way of Allah." This does not mean we should
hide in order to do inner battle — we must be willing at any
time to wage both the inward and outward wars. Otherwise, our
unification with Allah is superstitious, pseudo-Sufi nonsense.

These then are the stepping stones. Some of them lie on marshy
lands, and are very shaky in the ground. They are the despicable,
contemptible elements that make us sink. Some of them are
beautiful, firm little stepping stones in the middle of the ocean
of Allah's creation, and it is our duty to know which is which —
which stepping stones to avoid, which stepping stones to stand
on, on which ones we should occasionally stop and catch our
breath, and on which ones we should proceed quickly.

The answers to the above-mentioned questions all dovetail
into one another for they all are interlinked. Similarly, we cannot
take the outer divine law and forget the inner meaning. If we
did this, Islam would become superstitious religiosity, only a
veneer. It would then become only a ceremony, a piece of religious
celebration. Islam is real courtesy. If we are truly courteous,

then the outer courtesy will lead inward. We must pursue it, we must go and find out about it, and that knowledge is available. It is not difficult, provided it is explained in a manner that is compatible with our age, easily digestible and accessible.

The Prophet said to his companions, "If I tell you ten things and you forget one, you are in the Fire. However, a time will come when out of these ten things, if people remember only one, they will be people of the Garden." This is our time. So take heart, but do not use that as an excuse to be sloppy. Be careful, for the self is very clever. Be careful of hypocrisy for it is very elusive: it comes in and escapes through a hole before it can be caught. So catch it, block up that hole, truly reflect.

People today do not even have time to look at their own reflections in the mirror, let alone truly reflect. They rush here and there, from the womb to the tomb. Look at the traffic — half of it is going this way and half the other way. It is a crazy world with everyone chasing after their desires.

Life is full and you contain all of it, in a meaningful form, in your very breast. That is the meaning of the tradition related to the Prophet from Allah that "The heavens and the earth do not contain Me, but the heart of a trusting believer contains Me." In other words, a believer has in his heart the sub-genetically encoded seed of the meaning of the entire creation.

A start must be made. This start is like clearing a deep well that has been filled with debris from many years of negligence. Every person must dig out his own well, nobody can dig another's. All one can do is learn from others how they dug theirs, learn how they sharpened their tools. One must dig until the bottom is reached. Then the spring within will be found. We can only help each other courteously, correctly, and generously.

When we have cleared the well we will be fully alive and joyfully content, living in a manner that befits man, living on this earth without being swamped by it, without being buried under its minute to minute problems and anxieties which affect everyone as long as they are alive. How can we live a life that inwardly gives us a taste of freedom, yet be available at any moment to depart? How can we be responsible, do our jobs and perform our obligations, fulfil what we promise, act upon what we say, and at the same time increase our knowledge and wisdom about this world and the next, about the seen and the unseen, for the two are connected. The separation is alluded to only for the sake of description. The seen and the unseen dovetail into each other, the same way as the day and the night.

As Muslims, we begin with the assumption that there is one Reality, and there is no god except one God. First is negation and there is a great secret in it. We are programmed in our own lifetime to recognize first what is not. When we are young, very few of us know what we want to do, but we know much more clearly and much more commonly what we do not want to do. We know what is wrong, we know what is causing anxiety. We know that a certain neighbour has caused us trouble, we know that a particular type of boss, or job, or career is not desirable. We discover what is not, because it does not give us happiness, is not reliable and does not last.

Nothing lasts, neither money nor relationships. Even what one knows may be found to be insignificant. What is the use of knowledge if suddenly one is drifting upon an iceberg in the middle of the sea? What is the use of being a billionaire if one finds oneself in the middle of a desert with a crashed aircraft? Invariably one will discover what is not. What is not is any attachment, any connection, any desire, any expectations in the world. This discovery is made by suffering these expectations. The experience is common to us all. We have all experienced suffering from being attached to something — a child, a wife, a house, a coat, a car, or whatever.

That is why there is a secret in negation. Abraham, for example, as we are told in the Qur'an, negated the worship of the sun, the moon, and the stars in order to teach his people about the way of unity. Nothing lasts, and whatever we know of the world is of no use to us in entirely different circumstances, especially the circumstances after death. Then one discovers *la ilaha illa'llah* (there is no god but Allah). After the negation one comes to the affirmation. After having said, 'No, it is not acceptable, I will not be satisfied by these things,' when one is bereft, then the conclusion is reached by deduction that there must be a reality that encompasses all of these different things. It is a

natural conclusion, and is called knowledge of certainty. By deduction, through the faculty of reason, one reaches a conclusion
that there must be one Reality encompassing what appears to
be duality.

Life is balanced on pairs of opposites. Whatever state we are
in, it represents one of these two opposites. If we are quiet, it is
the opposite of being noisy. Thinking is the opposite of non-
thought. Being awake is the opposite of being asleep, and so on.
Often, in our actions in this life, we move from one end of the
spectrum to the other. We oscillate back and forth, either breathing in or breathing out, or suspended from two opposites, and
it is a puzzle. Our purpose in creation is to solve this puzzle, to
see what is really behind it, because two is not satisfactory. Two
is associated with other than Allah. We see two because this is
how the world is, and we are given the faculty of intellect and
discrimination as Adam was before his apparent disobedience.
It was not, in fact, disobedience because he had not seen anything
other than the truth. When he heard the voice of someone, he
looked at it simply as the truth, like a child in a sense. He was
a child in the garden of the Creator. Then he had to earn his
way back to that garden by differentiation and by discrimination,
by means of the seeds of wisdom, knowing when and how to act,
and, just as important, how not to act; how not to be deceptive,
and how not to be too clever, because cleverness has a level of
deception; how to be sincere by being in submission. The true
state of submission is a very difficult state to fully experience
and unify with because it implies a measure of helplessness, and
we do not like to be helpless. We all want to be active and
dynamic, we all want to experience things. Biologically we are
dynamic. Being in submission and also being active is a state of
knowing that one's actions will be in line with destiny and thus
will be successful. We will not go into that in detail now, because
it is a major topic encompassing questions such as, what is the
meaning of destiny? What is the meaning of free will? Is one free,
or not? Is everything decreed before it's occurrence or not?

Allah is in non-time, beyond time; He is the non-time dimension. Whatever we experience over thousands or tens of
thousands of years, whatever occurs cosmically over billions of

years, is wrapped in non-time, projected upon its fixed substratum, unfolding as events in time. We are able to experience time because there is the backdrop of non-time within us, and this allows us to measure time, allows the experience of time as relative. If we are happy, then time seems to go fast, but if we are unhappy or troubled, then it seems to drag. Imam 'Ali Zayn al-'Abidin said in a supplication: "Oh Allah, don't ever allow me to be arrogant enough to think that after I take this breath, another one will follow." He also said, "Oh Allah, forgive me if I ever think that by lifting one foot, the next will automatically follow." Look at the state of awareness of that great being. He was awareness itself. For him there was no past, no future, only non-time, only Allah.

The Qur'an says,

> So that you may not grieve for what has escaped
> you, nor be exultant at what He has given you.
> (57:23)

What does this mean? It means, do not be sorry for anything that is past and do not be excessively expectant or hopeful about things in the future. Do not dwell on past memories for this tarnishes one's energy now. Do not allow the past to be carried over to the present. If half of the time one is concerned about yesterday's wounds, half of one's energy today is unavailable. And if half of the time one is busy looking towards tomorrow, then half of one is not present to experience today. All our being present is not even good enough, let alone half. Be real, be now, be wholesome. This is *tawhid*, unity.

We are talking about different manifestations of this fundamental issue of the One and Only Reality — Allah, Glory be to Him, the Mighty, the Majestic. He is the Non-Manifest. We cannot describe Him or talk about Him. The Prophet advises us to talk only about Allah's attributes and actions. In this way we can get closer to that subtlety, because He is the Subtle. His is the Majestic Name. With Him is complete freedom and joyfulness.

For the people of Allah this world is a prison. Imam 'Ali Zayn al-'Abidin described death by saying, "When an unbeliever dies,

it is like taking off his wedding gown. When the believer dies, it
is as though he has removed a filthy robe which he had yearned
to discard." If this life is not viewed as a preparation, as the
place where we are polished in order for that diamond within
us to shine, then we have missed the point. We cannot talk about
Islam, we cannot talk about faith, and we have no right to talk
about the Prophet. Our Islam will become superstitious and it
will become something separate from us: once a week we will
go to a mosque, or we will bend our knees five times a day, or
whatever. The Prophet said, " For how many people does fasting
bring nothing other than hunger and thirst?"

The Prophet once heard a woman neighbour cursing her servant. He sent her some food, and she sent back a message saying
that she was fasting. He said, "How can you be fasting, and yet
curse your servant? What is the use of your fast?" We cannot
take just one portion of our path. We cannot take only the outer
practices without the inner meaning. What is the inner meaning
of fasting? The real meaning, the inner secret, is for one's heart
to fast from anything other than Allah. First, however, one must
refrain from the outer — sex and the stomach, which are man's
two weakest points. When Muslims become decadent, it is
through these two things. If one wishes to clinch a business deal,
one merely invites the other fellow for a sumptuous lunch. At
the end of the meal the man will be stupified from all the blood
that has rushed from his head to his stomach. Those who are in
business know exactly what we are talking about. First feed the
brute. Similarly, the intelligent woman knows how to get to her
husband — through his belly.

The recognition and awareness of negative habits allows these
tendencies to fall away. When a person genuinely recognizes
what they are doing, if they actually stand back and see the
damages, then they are more likely to fall into a cybernetic
process of self-awareness, rather than simply admit, in a clumsy
hypocritical way, that they are bad fellows.

Returning to the aspect of time, let us examine a small element
of the meaning of decree and destiny. We must approach this
meaning through linguistic definition. *Qadr* in Arabic means a
measure. *Qadas* means destiny, justice, judgement, what has pas-

sed. *Qadas,* which is destiny, comes according to *qadr,* or measure. It is scientific. There is no such thing as luck. The outcome of an event will be according to the measure of all the elements involved. As we know, a small element in life can change so many other elements. One person who refused to submit to the system of denial and disbelief in Iran changed the entire shape of world history. One person who abandoned himself and would not yield to compromises, because any small compromises at certain crucial times can be complete compromises. Ayatollah Khomeini knew that there were certain elements that had to be removed. The entire nation of Iran was basically Muslim but they had lost their Islam, it had become diluted. The removal of one key element, the Shah, who was the agent of corruption, was needed. How can one compromise about identifying where the evil lies? Ayatollah Khomeini had no means at his disposal when they sent him a message inviting him to come, but he said he knew that he was as low as he could go and the Shah was high, so what is high must come down and what is low must rise. All it takes is the interlink between different elements which we cannot always measure. Could anyone of us eight or nine years ago have predicted what was going to happen? Ayatollah Khomeini was unknown to most of the world at that time. All the great powers were helplessly paralyzed.

Everything that happens does so according to elements that interact upon each other, and the result is destiny. What is one's destiny, then? One's destiny is subjective individual experience, compared with the rest of the orchestration of surrounding events. If one's intention to perform an action coincides with one's overall destiny, then the result is perfect harmony. We have all heard or know of people who withdraw and shut themselves away from the world. Occasionally we also experience that feeling of not wanting to get out of bed. This is because our wishes or desires have too many times been blunted against our overall destiny, and failure was the result. Not wanting it to happen again, we become paralyzed. But who told us to have those desires? Why are we not intelligent enough to know what is written for us? This is why we want to know Allah.

Do not take our traditions lightly for they expound the know-

ledge of Allah. They are total, they are absolute, if they are
authentic, if they are from our Imams and the Prophet. They
provide more detail for what is already in the Qur'an. There are
two types of knowledge, one is informational or technical, such
as how to weave a cloth, sew a dress, or drive a car, and the
other is divine or revealed knowlege. Self-knowledge is part of
the latter and it is innate. One must cultivate it. We spend too
much time and energy on informational knowledge, which is
worldy knowledge, and thus, we are all out of balance. Man
is made of both soul and form. The body must be cared for
moderately, not too much nor too little. The soul is the same.

Listen to the voice of Reality, the voice of unity. Allah says
in the Qur'an:

> Do men think that they will be left alone on saying,
> We believe, and not be tried?
>
> (29:2)

Do people think that they merely have to say that they are in
complete trust and faith to avoid being afflicted and tested so
that their true state may be known? Was I here to gain some
acknowledgement, some joy, or money, or what? Or have I come
here without any expectations whatsoever? It is Allah's mercy
and Allah's proof that no matter what one does, it must be faced
and the intention also will be reflected in it.

The Prophet, talking to Abu Dharr said, "Act as though you
see Allah; whilst you may not see Him, know that He sees you."
We know that even though we do not have a concept of that
Reality which is in non-time, we will taste an aspect of the
attributes when we die. So we must have death in front of us at
every moment; by this, we will be far more alert.

Think of arrogance and anger. Wouldn't they become less if
one suddenly remembered that at any moment one might die?
Think of death, think of non-time, and your perspective will
change. Time will stop. There is no guarantee that you will not
die at any moment.

We have the freedom to choose how to live. We have the
option of living according to the divine way, according to Allah's
decree. In this way we will end up unifying our will with destiny,

and we will live freely, and yet as slaves. Look at the word 'slave'. In Arabic it is from the same root as the verb ' *'abbada* ' which means to pave a road so that it is smooth and serviceable, so that it has no resistance. The true slave has no resistance; there is no difference between him and his master.

We have a choice. We can act in a manner that is not going to add more to the egoistic qualities of arrogance, vanity, expectation, and desire or we can act in a way which will enhance and cause these qualities to grow. If we desire the former, then we have only to observe ourselves. We want everything to collect, or to become kings and queens — by nature we want to control. It is the echo of the Controller within us. We want to imitate Allah. Everyone imagines this at some time or another.

Let us look at this thing called arrogance and what the result is. The Shah was pumped up in the end, pop! The Arabs entered Jerusalem as Muslims and they were kicked out as dogs. And look what has happened to Arab nationalism — no two Arabs can agree on anything, because they have fallen into that low, animalistic thing, nationalism. And they talk about Islam! True, there are Muslims among them but this has nothing to do with Islam.

A Muslim is a person who recognizes that there are prescribed limits and that he also has the freedom to act correctly. He has the possibility of distinguishing correct from incorrect action, and because our life is short, those of us who have sensitivity and want to succeed want to then imitate the Prophet, and follow in the dust of his footsteps.

There is a story of an old man from Medina who was in his late eighties. His feet bled, he wore an old, long trench coat which had been purchased third-hand. Another man who had come to Medina to visit the Prophet's tomb saw the old man and felt compasion for him. He went up to him and asked, "Could I buy some shoes for you?" The old man answered, "How could I wear shoes? I do not know whether the Prophet himself stepped where I am stepping? How can I ever step with shoes upon a place where he may have stepped?" Consider this man's love for the Prophet, and the secret to following him will emerge. If one is truly in Islam, he must think to himself: 'Does this place I am in, this way I am acting, conform with what the Prophet would approve of? If the Prophet were passing by and came to your home, what would he say?' Would he stay with you? Are you his friend? Do you love Imam 'Ali? What would 'Ali say if he came to your house? What is your relationship with your wife and your children? What are you doing for your children? When we do not ask ourselves these questions, Islam becomes superstitious with no real meaning.

We must find out what things mean. Why are we here, why do we resent some things and like others? What is our innate nature? What is our origin? Who is our Lord and Sustainer and how can we follow Him? Those are the issues. Let us solve the major issues the ignorance of which causes us trouble, for there is no outward problem to solve, the problem is you and I. To solve the problem we must dissolve its locus.

The Prophet said, "Those who are nearest to you are the most qualified for your love." Who is nearer than ourselves? So first let us find out who we are? What are all these different states that we go through? How can we stabilize? We love stability. How can I be completely centred and content and yet remain active? Look at the Prophet's dynamism; look at the life of 'Ali. A man who was willing to behead anyone who was a true enemy of truth and at the same time was the gentlest, the most compasionate and the most considerate among men . The quality of a person cannot be improved without moving away from the lower qualities of the self. One cannot go higher without leaving the lower. One cannot become more concerned about real life and its future unless one gives up concern and obsession for this world. If one is concerned about others, then the focal point of mischief and harm decreases. It is displacement. One cannot take just one aspect of Islam and say, 'That is enough for me.'

> Allah does not impose upon any soul a duty but
> to the extent of its ability; for it is (the benefit of)
> what it has earned, and upon it (the evil of) what
> it has wrought.
>
> (2:286)

The worst thing that has afflicted Islam is modernism. There is nothing modern about it. Islam is about divine revelation, about obedience to what is impossible not to obey. If one disobeys, one is broken. If Allah loves someone, he is broken immediately at the very moment that he does something wrong. The people who never get caught are far away from Allah, and they too will have their moment of being caught

> And affliction is combined with affliction; To your Lord on that Day shall be the driving. So he did not accept the truth, nor did he pray, But called the truth a lie and turned back.
>
> (75:29–32)

Improvisation and modernization are not possible — there is nothing new.

14

The Ecology of Unity

In the beginning, we do things for ourselves, then for our families, then for our society, for Islam, and ultimately for Allah. In the Qur'an it is the righteous who say:

> We desire from you neither reward nor thanks.
> (76:9)

If one's intentions and the actions which emanate from these intentions have no expectations, and no reward is expected, the result is joy, for the action is done purely for its own sake and the reward is in the action itself regardless of the result. This pattern of living begets the most amazing bliss, and becomes more and more habitual. In fact, one becomes greedy for spiritual bliss, and that is a wonderful greed. One becomes envious of those who have more of this bliss and that is a wonderful envy. One seeks the company of the lovers of Allah. The Prophet said, "Whoever keeps the company of a people for forty days, becomes one of them." This is because a person must connect ecologically. Everything is based on unity. Nothing can remain in isolation.

The state of the believer is that he has no yesterday. Yesterday is buried. He is present to the here and now. He is aware, aware of whence he has come and whither he is going. All the time, with every breath, with every heartbeat. Thus, yesterday is not relevant. We have all made mistakes yesterday — finished, let's get on with it.

Look at the mercy of the divine law. A man's hand may be cut off because of a theft he committed, but one cannot call him a thief, because the punishment has already been done. He has paid his due. One must deal with him, look at him and yet not be shocked, because that was yesterday. He cannot be treated as a second-class citizen. Look at the greatness of this path, the outer and the inner connect, there is no separation. If the outer does not help the inner, if the prayer, the fasting, and pilgrimage to Mecca do not help one to be free of heart, then something is wrong. The path to Allah is unity.

We will explore a few verses of the Qur'an in order to more fully recognize how important it is to have knowledge, for true knowledge is obtained by going back to the real source. We must live in the garden of the Prophet, and doing so we will be with the people of his house, the selected companions; thus we will be under the shade of the Qur'an.

> Surely conjecture does not avail against the truth at all. Therefore turn aside from him who turns his back upon Our reminder and does not desire anything but this world's life. That is their goal of knowledge.
>
> (53: 28–30)

Imagination or one's opinion does not replace absolute truth. How do we remember Allah? By remembering His attributes, the First, the Last, the Inward, the Outward, the Living, the Self-Sustaining, and so on; and by leaving those who do not remember — "turn aside from him who turns his back upon Our reminder."

Part of Allah's affliction upon us is to test and strengthen our faith through people and situations that do not enhance His remembrance. Moses left his people for a short time, forty days, and when he came down from the mountains, the Israelites were already in a state of chaos. They were worshipping an idol, an object of gold. He became angry, but immediately recognized,

> It is naught but thy trial.
>
> (7:155)

Thus, he remembered that it was Allah's plot and knew that he must accept it as a true slave. So leave it, leave it all; all life is a trial. Be careful, be awake, and for those who

> do not desire anything but this world's life, that is the goal of knowledge.
>
> (53:29–30)

The Qur'an describes the Prophet,

> And We have not sent you but as a mercy to the worlds.
>
> (21:107)

When the Quraysh chased him from Taif (a town near Mecca) with stones, he prayed like the Prophet 'Isa (Jesus), "Allah forgive them, they do not know what they are doing." They were behaving like children. See how children fight and squabble over a tiny little plastic toy, because they do not know any better. That is why grown ups will blast each other's countries to bits for no sensible reason, for the sake of a few buildings: with neutron bombs, all the people are killed but the buildings remain. If this is not idol worship, then what is? Idol worship is not only worshipping stone. Do not think that idolatry is a thing of the past. If this were so, then we could dispense with most of the Qur'an. The Qur'an is forever, for every time, and every occasion. There is idol worship even in our sophisticated age. For instance, there is a street called Rodeo Drive in California where buses take tourists. The street contains something like sixty to eighty enormous mansions, beautiful buildings. Outside lighting illuminates them beautifully at night, but nobody is inside.

All of these actors and wealthy people are either suffering from alcoholism and recuperating at a clinic somewhere, or they have run away with their mistresses to a secluded island. The buildings are empty, and automatic devices come on — the sprinklers, the lights, and so forth. Isn't this idol worship? Observe how people are when they take others to their houses to show off? This is more true for people who have not had anything in the past, especially people from the East. When they have made acquisitions, they all take you to look at their houses. A man becomes secure when he is near his house or office — that is his security because he does not know anything else. Idol worship prevails everywhere.

The Qur'an is a manual for existence, for survival from minute to minute. If it were not relevant now, it would not be worth preserving. One will find, however, upon proper examination, that every part of it is relevant to a special situation. The deeper one dives into the Qur'an, the more clearly this is seen. And the more one sees in it, the further one advances, until in the end nothing may be said except, "Allah, Allah." If one fails to perceive this, the point has been missed.

Another verse is:

> O you who believe! Answer (the call of) Allah and
> His Messenger when he calls you to that which
> gives you life.
>
> (8:24)

The beginning of the verse addresses those who believe, those
who know or who have trust that they will come to know. There
are levels of knowledge. In regard to this, the esoteric writings
of Islam speak of the knowledge of certainty *('ilm al-yaqin),* the
source of certainty *('ayn al-yaqin),* and the truth of certainty *(haqq
al-yaqin).* The knowledge of certainty is obtained by deduction.
If someone comes and says that there is a fire in the forest, one
then has knowledge of the situation if he believes the person who
has seen it. From his own knowledge of fire and forest, he com-
bines the two and suddenly sees the trees burning. An example
of the source of cetainty is when the man actually takes another
person and shows him the fire in the forest — so that he actually
sees it with his eyes. This knowledge is more certain. The truth
of certainty is when one actually burns in the fire. Our masters
also say that there is a fourth stage, called "the truth of truth"
(haqq al-haqq), which is to be truly in the footsteps of the Prophet.
To say, "There is no god but Allah" is easy, especially in the
West where they love Allah. But the difficulty is "Muhammad
is the Messenger of Allah". People do not want to accept that
because they think they are free and imagine this will constrict
them or will change what they are used to. They do not realize
that ultimate freedom comes from ultimate constriction. Knowledge brings constriction: the more one knows the more one is
constricted. The less one knows, the more one thinks that one
is free.

The verse continues,

> Answer Allah, and His Messenger when he calls
> you to that which gives you life.
>
> (8:24)

This implies that we are dead now, and that this is preliminary
to real life; real life being the awakening into divine knowledge.
"That which gives you life" is Islam, it is true submission and

abandonment, from which you cannot but act without expectations, free and yet a slave. Having obtained a general picture of the whole thing, one can dive deeper into every aspect, finding incredible gardens therein. Every door opens another thousand doors. One becomes more and more addicted to this experience, and one finds that one develops a degree of efficiency in worldy activities that was not previously there. Because one becomes so clear and precise, five minutes of active life or planning will result in far more than hours of hard work before. That change of attitude towards the Hereafter will bring about this element. It is the fulfilment of Allah's promise — a tradition from Allah *(hadith qudsi)* says. "If you take one step towards Me, I will take ten steps towards you."

No one will be deprived of anything that they have. We had nothing to begin with anyway. We were never asked whether or not we wantd to come to this life. The whole affair is not ours, but we imagine that it is. We are like a child who has something in his hand. Try and open it, and there is resistance. However, once the child has learned how to relax his hand, and accepts that the thing will be taken away, his hand opens wide. But we must test this for ourselves. Do not blame others, for the buck stops with us.

Everyone is responsible for himself,

> Nay! Man is evidence against himself,
> Though he puts forth his excuses.
>
> (75:14–15)

We bear witness against ourselves though we may have a million excuses: 'Not now, not until I have my situation sorted out, until I have my family situation secure, and then I will ... .' How does one even know that he will live until tomorrow? How can one say, ' I'm going to sort out my affairs, I just want to make my family secure first.' As though the path of Islam is going to rob you of this experience in the life of this world. So many people, especially from the East, say, 'But this is very difficult, I must become secure first.' What is the use of wealth unless it increases one's faith? And how can one be increased in faith unless one is increased in abandonment to Allah? Ultimately wealth belongs to no one anyway. The Muslims use the tradition, "The stronger believer is better than the weaker one" as a rationalization to acquire wealth. Many so-called Muslims use what sounds correct, but in the wrong context. Like Mu'awiyyah, for example, at the Battle of Siffin: when he was about to be defeated by Imam 'Ali, he lifted up the Qur'an and said, "Let the Qur'an be the arbitrator between us." Many of those fighting with Imam 'Ali had memorized the Qur'an, and when Mu'awiyyah's men raised up their Qur'ans, Imam 'Ali's men confused their reverence for the Qur'an with the physical book and would not continue fighting. They did not realize that Imam 'Ali was the Qur'an on two legs, the living Qur'an. Mu'awiyyah was a trickster. People asked Imam Ja'far as-Sadiq if Mu'awiyyah had intellect. He replied, "No, he had *shaytan* ." It was not intellect *('aql)*, for intellect causes one to worship Allah and causes one to avoid the Fire.

The Qur'an says,

> The evil of their deeds is made fair-seeming to them.
>
> (9:37)

They think they are right. Also, the situation is cybernetic. Any correct movement will feed itself, and what is incorrect will also feed itself. Each situation, right or wrong, will have its justifications. This is the law of Allah. One who has no claim upon life is fully alive, because he is then acting and not reacting. Most of us react. Something comes from the outside, it is processed, and we react to it, wanting to preserve the good and avoid what we consider to be bad. After giving up all claim the individual ceases to react. If he is not certain, he may take counsel or wait patiently, acting in his own time. The person who acts is not constantly trying to catch up. These are all the ultimate fruits, the ultimate outcome, of true faith.

The Qur'an says,

> Is he who was dead then We raised him to life, and We made for him a light by means of which he walks among people, is he like him whose like-

ness is that of one in utter darkness whence he
cannot come forth?

(6:122)

Light means the light of knowledge, the knowledge that he lives
and works in a manner that is not going to cause problems. That
is effective and free action. Such a being believes that this experience here is only an experiment to reveal his own state. It is a
wonderful test. You love your beautiful child, and yet you must
not fall into the trap of believing it is yours. We are the only
guardians. Allah has given us all these props so that we may
remember, otherwise, we may fall into the trap, and become
emotional, and a most wonderful gift, this free gift of a child,
will become a burden, bringing fear and anxiety, instead of leading to the worship of Allah.

And whoever is blind in this (world), he shall also
be blind in the hereafter; and more erring from
the way.

(17:72)

There is no blind faith. Allah works through His creation so
there is cause and effect. We want knowledge, in fact we are
programmed to seek knowledge. As the child develops, he wants
to understand things. That is why he puts everything in his
mouth. He is actually announcing unity. At such an early de-
velopmental stage his experience is mainly oral as this is what
drives his to seek nourishment. Later on as he grows up, he seeks
to make sense of the world in every way.

Say: Are those who know and those who do not
know alike? Only the men of understanding are
mindful.

(39:9)

Only people of inner core, not those whose hearts are engulfed,
closed, or hard, remember what is this thing called heart? The
word for heart in Arabic is *qalb*. The root of it is *qalaba* which
means to turn, never attached, never stuck, revolving, free. Once

the heart is attached, it becomes sick.

> Has there come upon man any period of time in
> which he was a thing unrememberd?
>
> (76:1)

There was never a time in which we could not be remembered. We were in the memory, or in the knowledge of Allah. We were not in the knowledge of our parents. We were previously in the non-time zone, and that is why the tradition says that people who love each other in this life are people whose souls were close to each other in the past. Those who do not love each other keep away from each other. These things are real, polarity is real. This is the puzzle that we are here to resolve but this can only happen if we dissolve in submission. A point will come when the faculty of reasoning is no longer helpful. We can only go so far with our intellect and discipline. From then on, they must be abandoned.

The way of all the prophets and the way of all the men of Allah has been abandonment. Physically also they isolate themselves, abandon the world, so to speak. According to our traditions, the last ten days of Ramadan is one good time when we may isolate ourselves in particular mosques, such as those in Mecca and Medina. One remains in such a place of worship for a minimum of three days, coming out only for absolute necessities. Besides, other retreats were and still are practised. The Prophet, as did others who followed him, retreated to a cave. The purpose of such a practice is to get close to the knowledge of the One and Only Reality. One must, however, be prepared for such a withdrawal. There must be the right measure of outer and inner health to be able to do it, otherwise, the practice is one of no use.

We have tried to pluck a few tiny flowers from the vast garden of Islam, using the Book of Reality. Imam 'Ali describes the Qur'an's levels in numerous ways. He says there is something for the common people, something for the elite, and something for the elect of the elite. The Qur'an may be read repeatedly and something fresh will be discovered every time. This knowledge can only be shared in small circles if people are tuned together. Otherwise, it sounds odd.

We must remember that at any moment we may be recycled. Have we used this body which we have borrowed from the earth properly? Has it been used as a platform for us to take off from? The more determination and zeal we have, the more can happen, and the more we can taste true abandonment from which we will derive increased energy to follow this path. From this our lives can only improve. It is not necessarily a question of leaving a job, nor is it running away from anything. The matter is about facing the real self, truly, so that the lower part of it will fall away, and the higher part will be nourished. One can only improve oneself on such a path. A tradition says, "He who seeks his portion from the next life, his portion in this life will pass by him and settle in a proper order, systematically." He who claims his share of the Hereafter, meaning his share of the knowledge of truth, will automatically gain his share in this world. Nothing will be lost. The key to discovering the reality of this is to test it.

Affliction *(fitna)* is a plot against one, to distract one, to test one's ability to become detached and rise above it, turning one's intention to Allah. From this comes freedom. Everything is a plot against one unless it is done for the sake of Allah.

The verbal root in Arabic for affliction is *'fatana'*. To understand some of the nuances of this plot, we will look at some of the meanings of the word. *Fatana* means to subject to temptations or trials, to seduce. So affliction seduces one and makes it easy to fall into its grasp. Also it means to torture or to deny, which is the state of one who is seduced by it. Infatuation, enchantment, captivation are other meanings which describe how affliction seduces one. A further meaning is dissension.

We see in this example how the Arabic terms reflect each other. One of them has a precise meaning whereas the others tend to magnify the specific. The effect is kaleidoscopic. Another example is the word for oppression or injustice *(zulm)*. A similar word from the same root means darkness *(zalam)*. Now, if one is in light, he will not be unjust. This is why Arabic is not an easy language to translate, and also why it is not acceptable for any one other than a true believer who has died in Allah to translate the Qur'an, the hadiths, or the spiritual writings of the great men of Allah.

Let us move on to a discussion of good and evil. Whatever we experience in this world is from us. The root of the matter, however, is from Allah. We are allowed to experience good as well as evil and we may choose which to pursue. Allah has given us choice, that is why man is higher than the angels. The angels prostrated to Adam. It is a wonderful thing for us to recognize evil, thereby knowing exactly how to avoid it. Evil is the boundary, the wall of the garden. There can be no garden without a wall. Inside is good, outside are weeds and trash.

> And Allah encompasses all things.
>
> (4:126)

This does not mean that Allah brings us evil now. We have *'aql*, the faculty of reasoning, by which we are programmed to hate evil. We are genetically and subgenetically programmed not to want trouble and evil, but the problem is that we mistake evil for good.

> Yet why did they not, when Our punishment came to them, humble themselves? But their hearts hardened and the Shaytan made what they did fairseeming to them.
>
> (6:43)

What fools us is that good actions are always difficult to start with but end in ease. Bad actions, on the other hand, are easy to start with and difficult in the end.

The question thus arises 'Can evil actions be attributed to Allah since He is the Creator of everything?' This is impossible, for the Qur'an says:

> The Beneficent God, Taught the Qur'an, He created man.
>
> (55:1–3)

First, the knowledge of the Qur'an was established. The Qur'an is discrimination *(furqan)*. The knowledge of the Book of Reality, the eternal tablet is within us. Then "He created man." What sort of deity is this that creates evil for man? He says in His Book:

> And My Mercy encompasses all things.
>
> (7:156)

> They have eyes with which they do not see, ears with which they do not hear.
>
> (7:179)

Allah has created evil for us to taste and avoid. Allah has not created evil for us to embrace, so that we may become its champions. Everything is from Allah, but Allah does not want evil for us: it is we who fall into this pit because of our ignorance. Allah beseeches us to experience, to obtain knowledge, and to ask forgiveness, so that we do not suffer. Evil is good for us if we are against it.

There is a hadith which says, "If Allah wanted goodness for a nation, he would make their awakening to be at the hand of their enemies." There is injustice on this earth because of man's ignorance. Do not consider the injustice of some people against others as being Allah's doing. This is not what Allah wants for us. It is on account of our ignorance that we have been subjected to those tyrants or those regimes or those terrible situations. Allah has given us an intellect to recognize our plight and resolve it. The root is from Allah, but in between there is someone who is interpreting it wrongly. Our duty is, therefore, to seek knowledge ourselves and to act upon that knowledge without any desire for reward or thanks.

15

In Pursuit of the True Knowledge

We all wish for the prolongation of life. However, long life does not mean much, nor does good health, tranquillity, or anything else, unless it is on the Path, unless it is to acquire the most important knowledge, knowledge of Allah.

In our traditions, simply asking for the knowledge of the Essence will get us nowhere. We have to seek the knowledge of Allah's attributes, of Allah's actions, of Allah's laws, so that we may guard against transgressing them in this world. Guarding against falling prey to the pitfalls of following our own whims will protect us from the reaction born of wrong action which we call punishment. Punishment is part of the love of Reality for us. The entire creation is based on love. The pain we occasionally feel is because the balance has been disturbed due to our ignorance, because we do not know how to unite our expectations and desires with Allah's decrees and absolute laws. We are bound to adjust to them, and that is the meaning of slavehood. We are enslaved to that truth, whether we like it or not. The sooner we submit to it — and this is the true meaning of Islam — the sooner we will come to know from our hearts where to stop and where not to venture. If we make a mistake, then we have acted upon a desire or whim.

The purification of the heart occurs degree by degree, and the way to this purification is by going against one's own personal selfish motives, desires, expectations, and so on. This is called the struggle of the self, *al-jihad an-nafs*. Maintaining this *jihad* constantly, and keeping diligently to the *shari'ah* (the body of Islamic law) as it has come to us, one eventually ends up being the free man who is a true slave. If you are a slave, you have no choice. If you have no choice, you are free. Choice is confusion. Enslavement is fusion. There is no other way to this purification.

One can only deal with what is in front of one at any given moment, at any given time, in any given circumstances, and that is all one can do. The next experience will take care of itself. What happens after that is not our problem now. Let us sort

out our problems here, in this existence. Let us cross this bridge
properly, courteously, with full honor, with full dignity, and with
full humility to the Magnificent One, the Omnipotent, in whose
eyesight we are nothing. The entire universe is nothing. There
is a tradition saying that if you take the entire cosmos, it is no
more than a ring thrown in a vast desert.

Allah says,

> The heavens and earth do not contain Me, but the
> heart of a believer *(mu'min)* contains Me.

So what a vast potential a human being has! That potential
cannot be realized unless his options are narrowed down — narrowed down to such a point that there is no more narrowness.
That is the meaning of *fana' fi'llah*, annihilated in Allah. These
are all terms or indicators, meaning nothing more than a state,
a taste. Once the state becomes a permanent condition of the
heart, then that heart is a true reflector.

If the heart is a clean and polished reflector, it reflects the
truth. The objective of all inner practices is to reach a point
where the heart is completely free of everything — completely
open. Outer sound, in the form of *dhikr* (invocation to Allah), is
utilized in order to bring about inner silence. When inner silence
comes, a situation occurs which is a very healthy and normal
condition for mankind, a situation of being able to reflect the
truth.

Nobody likes disturbance in this existence, because the Creator
has created it in perfect balance and harmony. We do not like
discord, because our life has sprung from a harmonious foundation, and is based on that harmony. Harmony, however, is not
possible without dissonance. This is why man is at a loss, for
dissonance must exist in order to show us the bounds of harmony.
Finally, a stage is reached when the dissonance is not felt as
dissonance but only as harmony.

Today someone stopped us in the traffic. A woman who was
behind us pulled up alongside our car, lowered the window and
waved us down. I did not know what to do — I thought she
was telling us that we had a flat tyre. I was sitting in the front

seat, and lowered my window. The woman called out, "Who
are you? Where are you from?" I replied, "I am from the same
Creator and we are on our way back to Him." She said, "I have
been following this car, and there is peace and light in it." I
said, "Where is it that there is no peace and light?" Where is it
that Allah is not? What this woman recognized has become the
exception, the extraordinary, whereas, a time will come when it
will become the rule.

We are caught in that situation of no choice. We want peace,
we want harmony, and yet life is based on dynamism. This
situation seems a contradiction in terms, but it is not. The
dynamism of life has sprung forth from the perfect non-time, the
beyond-time state or essence which contains the dynamism that
sprung from it, but is not contaminated by it. That Reality is
not affected by what you and I can discern or observe or feel or
talk about. It contains it, yet is not impaired by it. He is *wahid
al-ahad*, the One and Only. We will all come face to face with
that dimension, that confrontation, when the potentiality of duality in this life disappears, which is the point of death. When
there is no more of this imaginary double — good/bad, up/
down, night/day, man/woman, health/illness — when this duality disappears, everyone will recognize the one foundation that
supports it all.

Adam could not have recognized the meaning of falsehood
until after Shaytan had told him to eat from the tree. Up to that
moment the Prophet Adam, that Adamic consciousness, had
only heard the truth. He did not know the meaning of a lie.
Once that occurred, duality necessarily became the foundation
of our existence — good and bad, up and down, lies and truth,
and all other aspects of duality. It is incredible, wonderful, and
perfect.

Let us share some verses of the Qur'an. We, as Muslims, live
by the Qur'an. There are two types of knowledge. One is knowledge revealed to the prophets, and the other is acquired, descrip-
tive, existential, encyclopedic, and informative. Revealed knowledge is thrown as light into the hearts of great beings — these
include 124,000 prophets, and many of those who follow in their
footsteps, if they have the courtesy not to disturb the dust of

these footsteps. The Qur'an is the ultimate revealed knowledge of Allah. It is a manual by which we live from moment to moment, just as we breathe in and breathe out. It is the ultimate manual for correct existence, not just a book to be brought out for major overhauls, like when somebody dies. It is for every moment, day and night.

The key to the Qur'an is with Muhammad and the *Ahl al-Bayt* (the People of the Household of the Prophet), and the *Sahaba* (his Companions). Full access to that revealed knowledge can only be obtained by means of those who were living with him. Otherwise, misguidance occurs or one may try to re-invent certain things.

I would like to share with you several *ayats* from *Surah Ya Sin*. Yasin is one of the names of the Prophet Muhammad, and his family or his tribe is Al-Yasin.

In the name of Allah, the Beneficent, the Merciful.

The Beneficent is the One whose mercy is all-encompassing. The Merciful is when one actually experiences the mercy.

> I swear by the Qur'an full of wisdom; Most surely
> you are one of the *mursalin* (Messengers of Allah)
> On a straight path.
>
> (36:2–4)

The straight line is the shortest distance between two points, and the ultimate objective is knowledge of the Creator. You will come to believe in Allah at first by simply accepting that He already contains all knowledge. He even contains the knowledge of one's existence before that existence comes into being. This is taken on trust until such time as you attain certainty of it.

> A revelation of the Mighty, the Merciful.
>
> (36:5)

The message has been brought down by the *'Aziz*. *'Aziz* is from *'izzah* meaning scarcity, power, strength. *'Aziz* also means rare, and dear, sought after as a result of its dearness.

> That you may warn a people whose fathers were
> not warned, so they are heedless.
>
> (36:6)

A prophet or a messenger comes in order to correct something that is going off its prescribed direction. No prophet, no messenger was sent to people who were completely and utterly on the path. Allah is not wasteful. Yasin was sent for those who wished to follow the path to knowledge of Allah. There is a hadith, a saying of the Prophet, that the men of knowledge are the heirs of the Prophets. They are the heirs of the Prophets because they love that knowledge. Through that knowledge they obtain life. The hadith also says that people are like walking tombs until they are enlivened. The Qur'an says,

> Therefore believe in Allah and His Messenger, the
> unlettered Prophet who believes in Allah and His
> words, and follow him so that you may walk in
> the right way.
>
> (7:158)

The Qur'an addresses those who trust that there is a purpose to this life. Those who trust that the inner joy and knowledge sought after is attainable, by exclusion — by excluding anything that is likely to cause trouble. That which has never caused harm nor ever will is already there. Exclude expectations, agitations, and desire. Leave all that aside. Know the mechanics of how these things arise. Automatically they will be left aside. Sometimes Shaytan is disguised in a good action, bringing doubt and trouble to the heart of a decent human being by joining him in his good actions. Observe how many people involved in charitable acts all of a sudden blow everything because they have not been properly acknowledged, or given their due respect. This occurs because Shaytan slips in where there is weakness. Usually one becomes vulnerable when one is not fully alert. Generally speaking, full awareness is not present when one considers oneself to be on a smooth path. On a smooth journey one generally encounters a sudden unexpected bump and Shaytan comes at moments when one is least expecting it.

Shaytan is, in a manner of speaking, very intelligent. A great *wali* (friend of Allah) was asked: "Who was your most brilliant teacher?" He replied: "Shaytan taught me, because he was more brilliant than all the other *'ulama* (scholars) whom I've come across. He was so brilliant that every time I thought I had caught him, he came up with a new set of horns, or way of doing the same thing." Shaytan is not just a funny thing; he strikes suddenly, and is very subtle. Anything that causes the heart to be tarnished, anything that causes doubt, is from Shaytan, no matter what it is. The believer must have discrimination, not doubt. If one doubts about a person or a thing, one is doubting oneself, one's own judgement, because of one's ignorance.

Basically, doubt and confusion are proofs of a deeper situation called anger. The power of anger turned against ignorance dispels it. If one's anger is turned against some other situation, blaming the stock exchange or another person, one is missing the point. If people look at their faults, they will never have time or energy to look at anybody else's faults. This applies at all times. You will conserve your energy because you will find deeper and more amazing things about the lower ego or *nafs* within us: how the *nafs* rises when one least expects it, how the *nafs* takes hold, guiding one towards a wretched abyss, under the guise of what appears to be nice and correct.

The believer must never be angry. If you are angry, then you are at a lower degree of *iman* (belief, trust, faith). The perfect believer as well as the perfect *kafir* (denier of the truth) does not exist. We all have varying degrees of *kufr* in us. *Kufr* is covering up, covering up the truth that occasionally we come to know and fully believe in, that there is only Allah, *la ilaha illa'llah, Muhammadun Rasulu'llah, 'Aliyun wali Allah* (There is no god but Allah, Muhammad is His Prophet, and 'Ali is the representative of Allah). That is the unquestionable truth that one whose state is right and whose heart is open can come to believe.

There is only one Reality. We are suspended by that Reality's grace in order to discover it, because it is beyond time, beyond place, beyond space, yet it contains space, and it contains us and everything which we know and everything which we do not know. As the Qur'an says,

> With your Lord alone shall on that day be the
> place of rest.
>
> (75:12)

This verse refers to the resting place of that Being, *Rabb*, whose job is *tarbiyah*, upbringing. *Rabb* is translated as Lord, making it almost meaningless. *Rabb* is one of the infinite attributes of Allah. Every speck of dust is an attribute, is an action, is an outcome of Allah's creation. We must recognize the fact that all prophets and all the messengers of Allah were sent to correct situations where there was a wastage of energy and lives.

The most precious capital that we have is our lives. Almost everything is potentially replaceable except the day, the moment that you now experience. For this leads to the Day of Judgement, the *Yawm ad-Din*. The Qur'an asks,

> Again, what will make you realize what the Day
> of Judgement is? The day on which no soul shall
> control anything for (another) soul; and the com-
> mand on that day shall be entirely Allah's.
>
> (82:18–19)

On the Day of Reckoning no self can help nor vouch for any other self. One is committed only to one's own inner state. The affair belongs to Allah. No action is possible. Another state of consciousness has taken over. If that state is attainable today, then a version of the Day of Reckoning has been tasted, because on that Day all that is hidden will be apparent, and all that is apparent will be like a shadow. This is the reverse of the present life. Nothing in existence can be experienced unless there is the reverse of it. Life is not possible without death. Sweetness cannot be experienced without bitterness. One cannot taste the amazing faculties of consciousness unless sleep is experienced.

We love sleep more than anything else in this existence. Sleep is a preparation for death. It is an acknowledgement of the fact that this body does not belong to us. We have simply used it for a little while, and we are returning it to where it belongs. So who then dies? How can the spirit die? Allah says,

> And they ask you about the soul. Say: The soul is
> one of the commands of my Lord... .
>
> (17:85)

Our spirit lives on forever, free, beyond anything, because it belongs totally to its Creator. Therefore, in its slavehood it is utterly and absolutely free — beyond time. For that reason, the believer is never afraid of death. For him it is the most natural thing, and can occur to us at any moment.

We believe in foreverness. We believe that Allah is *al-Samad* (the Eternal). The reason why some people of insight and inner knowledge do not want death is because there is something within them which suggests, in an indirect way, that there is no death. But they do not know what this state beyond the death of the physical body means. The believer, the *mu'min*, knows what it means.

The believer is never angry. Anger is a tremendous power. Lust is a tremendous power. All of these emotions and instincts are incredible powers, but they must be channelled correctly. Lust must be sublimated beyond physical lust, in pursuit of knowledge, in pursuit of a state of inner joy that is beyond description, an inner freedom that can only be attained by those who have the necessary fortune and forbearance and perseverance. If you have tasted it even for a moment, then you are hooked. It is like a drowning person who, while struggling, occasionally forces his head to the surface of the water. He tries with all of his strength to remain above water, but there is a courtesy necessary to enable him to keep his head permanently out of the water. The path is based on courtesy. Simply by moving one's leg, one is not going to swim in the current of life. Simply desiring to keep one's head above water, is not going to make it happen. Desire is necessary but one must also find a *wasilah*, a way, to make sure that his heart is where it belongs and his body where it belongs. His body belongs to this world, and what is inside, his heart, belongs to that world which contains this world and all other worlds, beyond time. If you have understood that, then you are truly born, then you are in balance. Then you can qualify as a human being, as a true slave of Allah. From this point on your life begins, because although outwardly you see affliction, duality, turmoil, and trouble, inwardly you are in the ecstasy of knowing how these things arise.

It is utterly simple. It is not complicated. It is not an intellectual exercise. It is not a matter for debate. It is. You either do it or you don't. If you do it, you get hooked to it, because the beginning is the beginning of the end. So Allah sends these Messengers, *anbiya*, to people who have lost the way, like us. That is why we need the prophethood of Muhammad.

We need to hang on to what the Qur'an reveals. We need to live by the Qur'an, moment by moment. If we are foolish, if we have acted foolishly at a moment of high inner inspiration, then it is we and no one else, who are to blame. Luqman advises his son, "Do not open your hand fully, and do not withhold it fully." Be in balance, so that you do not blame anybody later on. Someone suddenly has his heart opened, and becomes overly generous. It is a mood. Later on he blames those to whom he was generous for one reason or another. He was caught by his mood. It was a good mood, but do not blame anybody else. What we want is a state, not a mood. A mood of generosity is a spark of the Creator, because He is the most generous; everything is from Him, and it is to His grace that we shall all ultimately return. Allah's reservoir has no end. It is your reservoir and my reservoir that have limitations. We give a little bit and have expectations of a certain return or result.

> (As for) those who believe and do good, they shall
> surely have a reward never to be cut off.
>
> (41:8)

The Qur'an speaks about the people who have attained that state, not a mood. Be careful of generous moods. That generosity may be the worst thing that one is doing. Suppose a mood of pity or generosity comes upon someone for a child who has a very bad kidney. If one does not know about the child's condition, one may buy him chocolate candy. This shows a lack of discrimination. When there were plagues in the sixteenth century in England, the men of the clergy generously collected everybody under one roof. They did not know that they were actually speeding up death by doing so. Those who were not within the purvey of kindness of those ignorant people survived.

A true, pure action is *fi sabili'llah* (in the way of Allah), and actions in the way of Allah are for the sake of other people, for

Allah has no need for our actions. The Qur'an says,

> If you do good, you will do good for your own
> souls, and if you do evil, it shall be for them... .
>
> (17:7)

Thus, the believer never imagines or thinks that what he has
done in a moment of generosity was wrong. If ever one performs
a good action and later has second thoughts about it, then that
good action was not in the way of Allah. If it was peformed with
the right intention, then your reward will come from Allah, and
how do you know what Allah's measures are?

This morning we spent some time with an incredible being
who came to visit us. He is an incredible man of inner and outer
knowledge — of devastating humility and insight. He looked at
me and said, "He who is riding is not the same as he who is
walking." This struck a cord in my heart — I had just spent
some time in southern California trying to reach people, many
of whom came from strong traditions of Islam, and I was very
disappointed. I just seemed unable to get through to these people,
and found their ways very confused. I wanted to make sure that
I had understood what this man had meant, so I said to him,
"People are enemies of what they do not know." He said, "Yes,
and they speak to people about what they can understand,"
implying that I was with people who were pedestrians, and I
had remained on my horse. This was not fair. I should have
dismounted and walked as well. If I had wanted to be in the
company of these people, it was discourteous of me to do otherwise. We must use discrimination. Disappointment means that
we are not properly differentiating. I had assumed that these
people were all from the East and thus would have the right
courtesy. One cannot take people at their face value.

Generally speaking, the majority of people in America who
have been born as Muslims in other countries are very angry.
They are disappointed. Let us explore this anger. To begin with,
why are they here? What was their purpose in coming? Have
they come here to gain technology? How can they refit technology
into an Islamic situation? It is a major issue. Many of these
people try to brainwash themselves, thinking, I have only come

to the West in order to get the best, and not the rest. That is impossible, the two cannot be separated without a great deal of discrimination and awareness.

We become too exposed and this results in our becoming enticed and agitated. Yet we want to be at peace. Everything calls out beckoning one to become a consumer. More and more — more of what? First this thing is obtained then that. Bolts, locks, insurance, maintenance contracts, and so on. How can one ever manage to obtain a moment of inner peace and tranquillity in a situation like this? How do people manage to spare a moment with their families? In America, women take three months off to have a baby and then place the baby in a 'kiddy depot' for 9–10 hours per day. Everything is treated as if it were a possession.

Our medical profession has become the same. The individual, this great being, the representative of the divine Creator, is treated exactly like any other mechanical object. More and more medicine is in the hands of accountants and lawyers. It has become big business, and soon those businessmen will take over. Doctors, who a few years ago were unpaid salesmen for drug companies, are now third and fourth class slaves to these intelligent businessmen. So human beings are treated like machines — input, process, output. There is separation, specialization, fragmentation. There is incredible insight into outer forms of knowledge, and for that reason specialization is necessary.

The Prophet said, "There is a lump in a man's breast. If it is well, everything is well. And if it is not, then nothing is well." This means the heart, the purity or the state of the heart. Every one of us has outer limitations. What if one has inherited a limp or something similar? Everyone has his own idiosyncrasies, but we can live with them. The key is the state of our hearts. Prophets were sent in order to remind people why their hearts had become hard, what had brought them into that dreadful state. They came in order to tell people that they had transgressed the laws of the Creator, often ignorantly and inadvertently, by being distracted.

Distraction brings about destruction. Every now and then, after weeks or months of staying on course, trying not to be distracted, I find myself completely off course. Once I rushed to my teacher and said, "I have followed your teachings, I would have been able to face you every moment for months, but for only two days I found myself off the track." He replied, "You are speaking like a person who says, 'I have driven on a highway completely alert for ten hours, and slept for only ten seconds.' Those ten seconds would see you to the grave." One second of *ghaflah* (distraction) is enough.

If a person is unable to open his heart and keep things within his heart, they accumulate there, and in the end they cannot be easily washed away. A sledge hammer is needed to break through. Those who are on a strict path know what I am speaking about. Those who have occasionally taken someone under their wing, or helped another fellow traveller on this short journey, know what I am talking about. Suddenly one sees someone, and says, my goodness, what has come over him? His face has completely changed. The reverse can also happen. For someone who has a hardened heart, light may hit the heart through a small crack, and quickly the whole shell shatters and a being is born.

The Prophets come in order to warn people what went wrong. Two days ago we were reading about the Prophet Noah. The name *Nuh* in Arabic is from the verb *naha*, 'to cry'. He cried for his people. He was with them for 950 years, according to the Qur'an. He wept because they would not listen. He was trying to tell them that what they were doing was bringing about an ecological distrubance, which in turn would bring about their physical destruction. They had disturbed the cosmos to such an extent that it was going to flood. The consequences of one's actions will undoubtedly appear. There is no disconnection in this world. It is a complete jigsaw puzzle, and every bit fits. The great being who was with us today said, "If the head of a needle refuses to be what it is, the entire cosmos will be destroyed." This means that all of these powers and forces in the cosmos are so delicately and perfectly in balance, that not a thing can be disturbed without a reaction. The Qur'an says,

> ...then look again, can you see any fault?
>
> (67:3)

Look again, do you see any crack? Yet much of the time, either in our heart or our intellect, there is a crack that causes a lack of comprehension or discrimination.

The intellect is for differentiation, the heart is the connector to the source of differentiation. The head is for consciousness — to be conscious of this, that and the other: right and wrong, correct behaviour and incorrect behaviour; positive dynamism and action and being simply negative and aimless backward. The source of discrimination is in the intellect, in consciousness — which ascends higher and higher until one reaches pure consciousness. The root of the intellect dwells in the heart. Thus the saying, "Have a warm heart and a cool head." Warm means connected to the power source. Cool head means being a witnesser, to differentiate, to be objective.

One cannot be objective if one has attachments, expectations, and desires. The prophets came in order to guide people to the way, and the way has been and always will be one. It is called the way of submission, of Islam. Adam was the first and we will not be the last. There will be others who will discover the same thing. What differed from one prophet to another were the the outer limitations prescribed. Each prophet brought greater outer restraints — stricter, narrower — to make it easier, more immediate. The more specific the boundaries, the less choice one has. Ultimately, with real knowledge there is no choice. If one knows what the right ambient temperature should be for a room, there will be no choice between 20 degrees or 21 degrees. One knows it is 20.3 degrees. If one is offered a plate of various fruits, there appears to be a choice. If, however, one knew exactly what his system needed in order to be restored to its full balance, there would be no choice. He would take three and a half grapes, one and a half bits of apple, and everyone would think he was crazy. But he has no choice, because he has come to realize exactly what is appropriate for his condition.

When we say we have a choice, we mean we are ignorant. The more ignorant we are, the more choice we have. It is like a small child who does not know. He has all these choices, but as he grows older he finds that he has little choice. Ultimately, if we have inner insight of pure consciousness, we have absolutely no choice. That is the freedom that the prophets have come to teach, the freedom of no choice, according to the different circumstances of their people. There were prophets within one family, and there were prophets for a village. There were prophets who had their prophethood for a few moments, and others who had it for hundreds of years. The source of prophecy for each one was from the same divine spark. They carried the same message, in a different language, in a different era, until the Prophet Muhammad, Yasin, came to a people, the Arabs, who had experienced no prophet among them since Isma'il. It so happened that he was the last and the Seal of the Prophets.

The Prophet Muhammad's message includes the outer application, the *shari'ah*, as well as the inner way. The inner and the outer are one, as they are only two sides of the same coin. You cannot have an outer condition without an inner state. An inner state cannot come about or be tasted unless there is an outer condition. His way was the most perfect, because it was the most direct, the easiest, and most applicable at all times, in all circumstances, no matter where one is. One may live by it safe and sound in any place or time. By the Prophet Muhammad's way, one may live in this world inwardly as though one is in the Garden of eternity, whereas outwardly one may be striving and struggling. There is access to an inner state that is beyond description. That access can only come about if the key is manufactured. The key is based on battling with oneself, thrashing it out. If the self wants something, do the opposite. If the self is lazy, give it a push. When you go to a place where there may be a useful situation, the self will balk at going. At night, if you suddenly awaken, get up and pray the night prayer even though the self wants to turn over and go back to sleep. The reward of such actions is immeasurable. There are rules about how to perfect the self. Once these are practised, one is able to go further and further.

The prophets have all come to remind man that what he should be striving for is already there. It is only his ignorance, his self-delusion and the whims of the lower *nafs* which deprive him of this knowledge. Put the lower *nafs* aside, and ascend higher with the higher *nafs*, until neither high nor low is seen.

Only the manifestations of the One and Only Reality are seen. Then one is in the station of true submission.

The great man of knowledge with whom we spoke today said that Imam Husayn was in that state of submission on the day of his martyrdom. So think how miserable our state is. One should never imagine that one has attained the goal, for even a child can tell that one does not know. The knowledge which we are talking about is not a knowledge that can be discussed in words. It is *haqq al-yaqin* (the truth of certainty). It is the certainty that *la ilaha illa'llah, Muhammadun Rasulu'llah* (There is no god but Allah, and Muhammad is the Messenger of Allah) is true even if you are cut up into bits. Every bit, every cell, will sing *la ilaha illa'llah, Muhammadun Rasulu'llah*. That is what the prophets have come to give. This is what our Prophet Muhammad brought in the Qur'an through the medium of this most incredible language — the Arabic language.

To understand the Qur'an, one must do so through the medium of its language. There is no other possibility. Then one realizes

> Certainly the word (decree) has proven true regarding most of them, for they do not believe.
>
> (36:7)

The majority of people are the type who will not come to know the true message. They will not come to this realization, to this *iman* (trust, faith, belief). *Iman* is its own fuel, its own reward. The believer is in a state of trust at all times, so that even when something hits him and he does not know what, his trust in Allah will reveal to him what is happening, and will immediately put it right. If he is acting in the way of Allah, then he has removed all obstacles. Where is the problem? Why should he be upset? He can only be upset with his ignorance, for misapplying his energy at the wrong time in the wrong place. Those who are at a loss are described in the Qur'an:

> Surely We have placed chains on their necks, and these reach up to their chins, so they have their heads raised aloft.
>
> (36:8)

These are the chains of the drudgery of *dunya* (the material world). I must do this, I must do that. People become choked. The world has gobbled them up. They have no time. Their altar is the bank and their high priest is the bank chairman. 'In gold we trust.' This is today's form of worship. They work like slaves in order to have one or two weeks of holiday. The word holiday is from 'holy day', but there is nothing holy about it. I would like to have a holiday all the time, all my life. Why not? Why only for a few weeks? To go to some overpriced place where one is only concerned about whether or not the fish is cooked properly or whatever. Then later the madness is relived by showing our neighbours photos or home movies. All this is fixated, dead.

> And We have made before them a barrier and a barrier behind them, then We have covered them over so that they do not see.
>
> (36:9)

People's own actions and ignorance cause them to become disconnected. Every one of us is the product of his past. Every one of us, in our bodies and in our thoughts, is a mixture of our physical, genetic, environmental, and social material mixed together in various permutations and combinations. The outcome of it is the so-called individual self. If we do not recognize how this has arisen, we are disconnected from Allah. If I cannot see that my illness or the weakness of my kidney is the result of a combination of factors — an inherited disposition and my ignorant abuse of my kidneys and so on — then I am at a loss. It is cause and effect. It is scientific, it is perfect. Once one sees that, there is no harm.

Knowledge of the situation allows one to see the blessedness of an illness. One is knocked down to be warned and revitalized. It is wonderful, it is perfection.

The past is a connector, bringing forth a result which is then projected into the future. So how can one escape from the past? By recognizing it and changing the present so that the future will be radically different in its essence.

The Qur'an says,

> Whatever is in the heavens and the earth has declared the glory of Allah and He is the Mighty, the Wise.
>
> (57:1)

Allah sees to the past. He is in non-time, beyond time. Elsewhere He says,

> The seven heavens declare His glory and the earth (too), and those who are in them; and there is not a single thing but glorifies Him with His praise, but you do not understand their glorification; surely He is Forbearing, Forgiving.
>
> (17:44)

Thank God we do not understand their *tasbih* (glorification). If we could hear all the atoms whizzing around, or catch every wave-length that travels through the air, we would be terrified. We would be shell-shocked, not able unable to move an inch.

Those who are disconnected do not know what they are saying, nor what they are doing. Elsewhere in the Qur'an it says that their actions will be nullified; their work will be of no consequence, and they will be recycled. Allah will bring together people who love Him and whom He loves.

Who loves Allah? He who loves the Messenger of Allah. There is no other way. In science, for example, one must be guided by those who have a greater scientific mind, training and aptitude. The same thing is true of revealed knowledge. It is revealed to those hearts which are the full reflectors. It is like the moon and the sun . Without those prophets, without that revealed knowledge, we would have been worse than animals, because animals are in another zone of consciousness. They live, sleep, eat, fornicate and die without worrying. So why are human beings worried? They do the same gross things but they worry. This indicates that they may sink lower than animals.

The Qur'an says,

> Or do you think that most of them do hear or understand? They are nothing but as cattle; nay, they are straying farther off from the path.
>
> (25:44)

They are like cattle but worse — more at a loss. Cattle at least know who is male and female. They also know where good pasture is. They seek to find good pasture, and are positive. Often man does not do this. Even when he knows something is good he may not do it because it is contrary to his *nafs*. Man punishes only himself. If he were normal he would accomplish what he has to do as best he can and wait for something better to turn up with a positive attitude. But something is amiss — either in his heart or intellect. One must accept what is offered and move on. Allah will have greater openings.

Allah's feast is infinite. If one is true and honest, the wind of destiny will lift him higher and higher until he does not feel being lifted, nor any height, nor any lowness. He will just seek to please Allah, and when he faces the creation he will be discriminating. One must be positive, honest, real, and care for oneself, for this is real caring. Charity begins at home — and where is home, other than in one's own heart?

Returning to *ayah* 9 of *Surah Ya Sin,* these people are covered over because their intentions and actions are separated. If intentions and actions are not in unity, one has no access to *tawhid* (unity). One has no access to the science of knowledge of the Oneness behind what appears diverse. Those who lack this science have no insight. They perform actions, and at the end of their lives they die lonely and miserable, with everyone waiting for their death in order to divide the remains of what they have left behind. There is a tradition from the Commander of the Faithful 'Ali ibn Abi Talib which, paraphrased, says, "You are collecting and collecting. Do you know who you are collecting for? It may be for the fellow who is going to have a good time with your wife after you die. Have you ever considered that?"

Do we care about what is going to happen to us after death? Do we know that we are going into another time zone, and that we will be stuck in it forever? Forever does not mean long — it is another realm of consciousness. How can there be time without non-time? How can there be a motion picture without a fixed screen behind it? The one cannot exist without the other. The fact that everyone longs for a good situation to last is a proof that an echo exists in us of that everlastingness, an everlastingness which is not transferable to this realm of consciousness where nothing can be fixed.

> All those who are in the heavens and the earth
> depend on Him; every day (instant) He is in a
> (different) state.
>
> (55:29)

We have the opportunity of a full experience in the melting pot of this world, in order to be prepared for another world whose rules are different. The rules are in a non-time zone, and life there will be dependent entirely on one's actions in this life, which are inscribed upon the soul. If one has passed through this life with a clear, utterly open heart, then naturally in that life one will be totally free in a garden of delight. If, however, one has moved in this life to a situation where further purification is needed, the experience is either in the Garden or in the Fire. It could be an improvement. The fire is a *mithal,* an analogy. *Jahannam,* the name of that fire in Arabic, is a bottomless pit, forever, which is repellent because we seek stability. The ultimate stability is the knowledge of Reality and this is the foundation of what we experience as duality. We must be armed with an open heart that is willing to reveal what is hidden in it, a heart that is willing to expose its intentions, to speak out, to speak up, to unveil itself, inwardly free, yet outwardly constricted. We should consider whether it is the right time, the right place, the right way, the right people to speak out without misunderstanding. Be careful not to do what I did, when this great man told me that there cannot be a rider and a pedestrian together.

The outer courtesy of Islam is that a person on horseback must greet a person who is walking, because he has the upper hand, he is more mobile, and a person walking must greet a person who is sitting. A person who is sitting must greet a person who is reclining. These are outer courtesies, and ultimately all outer courtesies lead to inner courtesies. If you start by strictly following the *shari'ah* (divine law), you will end up being inwardly revived.

There will come a time when the entire creation will be completely spiritually evolved. It is the promise of the Qur'an:

> And certainly We wrote in the Book (divinely re-
> vealed books) after the reminder that (as for) the
> land, My righteous servant shall inherit it.
>
> (21:105)

There will come a time when every being is free. They will not
be like us, hoarding and running from here to there. We are in
the middle, that is all. We are pressed, and occasionally oppressed, yet it is for our good. We are in the right time and in the
right place and in the right way. If only we could see it.

Birds of a feather flock together. Those who are outwardly
sober are inwardly drunk, and other poor people who have no
access to this must go and intoxicate themselves with firewater
that burns their stomachs and has untold side effects. We must
be watchful of what we eat, how we eat it, and how much we
eat. We should consider not only the nutritional content, but
also the *barakah* of the food. How can one eat food prepared by
a person whom one does not know? We want to go out because
there is no love in the house, because the house has no heart.
In the East, the heart of the house was the hearth, the fireplace
around which everyone would gather.

Where can we begin? Where will we end? How can we go to
the Qur'an, if we have not started with proper discrimination,
for it says,

> Most surely it is an honoured Qur'an,
> In a book that is protected;
> None shall touch it save the purified ones.
>
> (56:77–79)

Outwardly as Muslims, one cannot touch the Qur'an, especially not its words, unless one has performed *wudu'* (ablution).
However, this last verse also means that the purer your heart,
the deeper one may read into it, until the reading is from the
Divine Author Himself. One may obtain insights or glimpses
into the Qur'an, one may taste the cup of that wine, but to make
further progress, certain courtesies and disciplines must be acquired. The youngster must be trained. Nowadays, youngsters
are trained to drink wine before they are even in their teens, so
by the time they are twenty they are already alcoholics. Fourteen

percent of the adults of this nation are registered as confirmed alcoholics. If we can find another fourteen percent of the population like us to partake of this eternal wine, then we have done something worthwhile in this world. It is better than the intoxication of alcohol without any of the side effects.

For this one needs to be groomed, and that grooming is strict *shari'ah* (divine law), totally strict. We can get away with nothing. There is no action, no matter how small or trivial, that has no reaction. The reaction may not necessarily be in the same plane. Lack of generosity, compassion, and clemency will beget inner tortures such as an inner ulcer, or a hardening of the heart.

The Qur'an says we are the *khalifahs*, the representatives, of Allah. No creature has such a responsibility. We are here to represent the Divine Being who is here but does not appear to be here. We appear here. Once we accept this situation, then we accept the responsibility of keeping to the narrow way. We must lower the eye, and become less and less addicted to consumerism. The consumer is being consumed. He is engulfed in the fire of his agitations — the mass crisis of Christmas shopping.

We are the lovers of 'Isa (Jesus Christ). He said, "My feet are my donkey, the heavens are my cover, my hands are my slaves." This was a great, free being. He is described in the Qur'an as *Ruh Allah,* the Spirit of Allah. We are his lovers. Where is that incredible forgiveness which he had? It has become the twisted, tortuous bible and the gun business.

We are the heirs of all the prophets, the heirs of the final Prophet, Muhammad, may Allah bless him and his family. To know the situation of parents, look at their children. The gate to them is through their offspring, those who come later. For that inner knowledge of which we are the heirs, there is a proper courtesy, as there is a courtesy in this life for everything. That courtesy is love for our blessed Prophet, and this love cannot occur and be nourished unless one comes to know him.

Muhammad is known by what he said, how he lived, and through the mediation of those who fully absorbed his teachings, the *Ahl al-Bayt* (the people of the House of the Prophet). They had greater and more immediate access to him. If one lives as though, at any moment, he may appear, then one is in his company. Being in his company, one is then in Allah's company, and the meaning of this is something that one must come to understand. First, however, one must walk, even crawl, until such time as the heart takes flight. There are no shortcuts, and this heritage cannot be purchased except at one price: to sell oneself completely to Allah.

The Prophet marketed the most incredible commodity, unseen, untouched, unimaginable — Allah. The price for this commodity is one's willingness to let go of everything and die. By death one lives. The Prophet said, "People are asleep; when they die they wake up." He also said, "If you want to look at a dead man walking, look at me." This means that he was dead to that which appears to be real. He is dead to what is only true as a secondary truth — this physical existence — and therefore he is alive to Him who is ever alive, ever-living. This is the *din* of *tawhid*, the path of unity, all we have, and more than we can bear — certainly more than what the mountains could bear.

The Qur'an says that this gift was offered to the mountains, and they were shattered, but humanity accepted the trust. For this reason humanity is "in a state of loss." (103:2) Wherever you look, man is at a loss, because he has the potentiality of that ultimate, infinite, indescribable inner knowledge, and he does not actualize his capability. Thus,

> Allah is not unjust to them, but they are unjust to themselves.   (3:117)

The believer is outwardly courteous and inwardly in ecstasy. Outwardly, he will never be satisfied. How can a believer in action, struggling in the way of Allah, ever be satisfied? No matter what he does, he knows the potential always exists to do it better.

The believer lives amidst turmoil. The Prophet was in the greatest affliction. No prophet lived in leisure outwardly. They were all subjected to tremendous tribulations. On our Prophet's death-bed, an argument was sparked off. Only a few people were with him when he died. The Commander of the Faithful 'Ali, when he was denied his right as the leader of the Muslims as stipulated by the Prophet, was asked, "Why don't you rise up?" He said, "Show me forty men, and I will arise." He also said: "When I open my eyes, I see so many, but I do not see anyone."

This is the state of the believer who is an heir of the Prophet. Outwardly, there is affliction and turmoil. Inwardly, there is for him indescribable joy in the recognition of Allah's unchanging laws. The Prophet Muhammad was hit by arrows because the men ran away to loot. The law of gravity did not stop the flight of the arrows. The Prophet of Allah lost his teeth and was bleeding. They thought he was dead. What tremendous sufferings he endured. He also knew what would happen after his death, that power-mongers would take over the outward leadership of the Muslim community. The Prophet exiled Ibn Marwan saying, "This man is poison and a serpent, he must leave." When Abu Bakr came to power, Ibn Marwan's people exhorted him to allow Ibn Marwan to return. Abu Bakr said, "My master exiled him, how dare I allow him to return. I will exile him further!" When 'Umar came, again the same thing happened, so 'Umar exiled him even further. This man, Ibn Marwan, ended up being ruler of the Muslims and stood on the Prophet's pulpit. The Prophet foresaw all of this.

He who has access to the One who is beyond time will see things of greater weight than we can bear. The Prophet foresaw what would happen to Imam Hasan and Imam Husayn. He knew one of them would be poisoned and killed by the mouth, and the other by the neck. Inwardly, he saw the joy of the perfect laws of Allah. These are the afflictions of the men of knowledge. If men do not want to live according to the laws of Allah, they will inscribe their own hell on this earth. The believer is inwardly joyful, for he sees that the way of Allah will never change.

16

A Living Model

Imam Husayn Day

In every aspect of life there is an outer form and an inner meaning. They are always connected but not always in the right balance. If the form is not joined with the meaning, then the balance in existence has been disrupted. If we do not live according to what we say and teach, our lives will become barren. If the true message of Islam is not adhered to, in both its form and meaning, then it is a distorted message and will end up being yet another religion which is far removed from its source. Thus has the Islamic heritage become diluted and sloppily tolerant. Muslims have become easy-going, open-minded, or injudiciously understanding. The result is that our children are out of place and in the wrong place, at the wrong time, doing the wrong thing and we blame them or blame others for our misfortune.

Those Muslims who have inherited the legacy of the *Ahl al-Bayt* (the family of the Prophet) by birth must yet earn the reward of this legacy by practising the form of this great heritage.

Of little value is that which is inherited. It is often destructive rather than constructive. It is very fortunate that we have certain occasions to remember, to reactivate, and to relive, so that we become unified, as members of that mystical caravan from time immemorial — that began with the birth of Adam — which raises man to the ultimate potential in this experience of life.

Let us look at the Qur'an, that we may share the recognition of the responsibility that is upon our shoulders.

> Only Allah is your Protector and Guardian and His Messenger and those who believe, those who keep up prayers and pay the poor-rate while they bow.
> And whoever takes Allah and His Messenger and

> those who believe for a guardian, then surely the
> party of Allah are they that shall be triumphant.
>
> (5:55–56)

Most of us know the specific, historical reason for the revelation of this verse. Imam 'Ali was in the bowing position of the prayer in the Prophet's Mosque in Medina. A man came in asking for a voluntary contribution of alms. The Imam, while bowing, lifted his hand for the man to take the ring off his finger. Now there is a question here that we all have to settle. How could a man like Imam 'Ali be aware of the fact that there was a beggar, a man seeking material help in the mosque when we have a tradition that his state was so undistracted in prayer that his companions pulled an arrow from his leg? Shaykh al-Tusi described in *Kitab al-Shafi* the meaning of how these two qualities were combined in 'Ali. In short, he was the greatest of believers in his prayer, yet he was fully aware of what was going on.

We are here in this life in order to follow the caravan led by the blessed Prophet, and by Imam 'Ali, and Imam Hasan, and Imam Husayn, and the nine other Imams. We are here in order to be in Karbala. Not once a year, or once a month, or once a week, or once a day but beyond time, to be in that state.

If we want to belong to the party of Allah, to the party of the Prophet's House, there are several conditions for it, not like most other parties which one can join one day and from which one can withdraw one's allegiance the next. This party is based on behaviour, the science of how to be. It is concerned with beingness. We are brought into this world in order to learn how to conduct ourselves, how to be in glorification of Allah, how to be in Islam which is submission, unquestioning and total submission. This the meaning of *tawhid*.

Imam 'Ali was a man of *tawhid*. He was a man who was in this world and did not belong to it, a man who was cognizant of its totality. It was he who said, "You think you are a small universe and within you is folded up the entire cosmos." He was in a state of prayer and yet was aware of who was in front of him. This is the state of a man in total abandanmont, in pure, absolute consciousness, unified with the entire creation of reality.

This man was one about whom it was said: "He gives drink and drinks and yet is not distracted by his drunkenness." This drunkenness was due to joyfulness, this drunkenness was abandonment in Allah.

About this state Imam 'Ali said: "His joy in that state does not distract him from his beloved; nor is he distracted by the cup; nor is he distracted by life, by troubles, by goals, or by doing righteous deeds." His drunkenness of his joyfulness was under his control because he was a fully awakened being. He was in the state of completeness. He was the perfect man. He is the man whom we try to emulate, the dust of whose footsteps we seek to follow.

The culture of the family of the Prophet is a complete model, an entire reality. If we want to know aspects of the overall reality then we have no other option but to take to the path that has been trodden by those who have achieved knowledge of that reality. That is the only logical thing that any man with sense and respect for himself would do. As charity starts at home, it must begin with the individual. Entering that party, to be as though he were amongst the Family of the Prophet, to be in fearful awareness, aware of death at all times. One must be willing to face the next life joyfully, knowing that we have done our best and that there is nothing left except to see the face of Allah without any distraction as is invariably the case in this life.

The affliction of Imam Husayn is the affliction of each one of us, except that in our case, since we are not completely dedicated to the path of Allah, we do not see it as sharply as in the case of Karbala. We are all at all times confronted with tests and affliction.

> Do men think that they will be left alone on saying,
> We believe, and not be tried?
>
> (29:2)

The purpose of this test is to enable us to sort out that part of us that must be left behind, to be destroyed, that is to say, the lower aspect of the self. Thus, the higher aspects will become habit, and a way of life. Our affliction is, therefore, positive, that we may evolve and move higher and higher into that ultimate realm that leaves us at the final point of *tawhid*. Here one sees nothing other than the blessedness that comes from the Creator even though, when an affliction is experienced, we may not like it.

A man of submission sees nothing other than goodness in his life which comes to him from his Creator. If he dislikes anything he sees it as deriving from himself or as a result of his own ignorance. Therefore, he is content at all times with his knowledge and behaves outwardly as correctly as posisble, balancing between justice and peace.

We have all begun from the point of absolute peace, non-existence. We have come from the unknown, from a point that we cannot remember or describe, but the truth is that it was remembered in the knowledge of Allah.

> There surely came over man a period of time when
> he was a thing not worth mentioning.
>
> (76:1)

Every one of us is a part of the one and only jigsaw puzzle. The entire creation is entire because of all that it contains, and we are an aspect of it.

So trial and affliction, *fitna*, is for our own benefit, for our own training, because it helps us to evolve, and if it happens in a revolutionary way, then that evolution is faster. If we are afflicted and every door is closed, as was the case for Imam Husayn in Karbala, then we should praise and thank Allah for we truly must depend upon Him. At such a time we are given the opportunity to say and to act upon "There is no power nor strength except with Allah the Most High, the Mighty." We cannot turn anywhere. We cannot depend on our family, neighbours, or friends.

Year after year we are given opportunites to reach the point of Karbala experientially so that we can go beyond the description of the moment. Not everyday is Karbala nor every moment, rather Karbala is beyond time. We are already with the eternal martyr who turns the name of destruction upside down and causes it to mean everlastingness.

The affliction of Imam Husayn is our affliction. His affliction has always afflicted mankind. The outward condition of his affliction was a result of man's apathy and complacency. The Muslims reverted to their old social habits of nomadic life. In nomadic life there was a hereditary leadership, but ultimately it was based on the ability of the best man to raid and fight, to be cunning, and to exhibit the highest level of courage and adventurousness. Also, compassion and generosity were qualities considered important.

The way of Muhammad elevated that culture into a much higher form, into the only fitting way for a man to exist in this life. Everybody was given the opportunity to worship. A man in a state of *tawhid* (unification with Allah) does not even recognize that he lives in *jihad*, that is to say, fighting in the way of Allah. He does not wait for someone to come and give him the answers. He is in a state of inner, constant revolution. He is attached to the world. He is free and yet constrained by his Creator. He is leashed by a leash which gives him his freedom: the freedom of no choice. He does not have to wonder or think. It is not a process of thought that is in time — that is electromagnetically, chemically and otherwise biologically constricted. It is spontaneous, innate, and instinctive. It is by Allah, from Allah, to Allah, because he is a man of Allah.

An enlightened member of the Prophet's family, in our time, once remarked that the birth of Imam Husayn was not on his birthday, which was the 3rd of Sha'ban in the 3rd year after Hijrah, when Islamic culture was at its pinnacle. Rather it was really the 10th of Muharram in the 61st year after the Hijrah, because that was when he was born to live forever.

Imam Husayn was a man who had no option. He sought peace as we all do, but he had no option in what he did. He already knew in his heart what was going to happen, but yet, as a human being like all of us, he had to go through the forms still thinking that something might happen, that somehow the hearts of the brutes he was confronting might turn. He lived every moment in that moment. He did not abandon any possibility. He followed the entire model to the fullest extremity until he realized the truth of the prophecy and the truth of his destiny. By his blood the ever-blossoming tree of Islam is able to grow in our hearts.

That is the model of Karbala. To know that model we must

strive and go through it, and the master of that journey is the Prophet Muhammad. This is a state that we can, at all times, attain. Nothing ever changes. The pattern merely repeats itself and continues, until man is finally evolved to such a degree that he is ready for the final justice of the Imam al-Mahdi. After his appearance mankind will experience complete peace on this earth. Until that time we are in the process of evolving to a situation where everybody will live the justice that is inherent in his heart. Each of us is first and foremost the judge of himself, not judging others until he corrects himself.

The Prophet Muhammad said: "Injustices are of three types: one type is that from which we will never be forgiven and it is association with Allah." The Qur'an says about this:

> Surely Allah does not forgive that anything should be associated with Him, and forgives what is besides that to whomsoever He pleases; and whoever associates anything with Allah, he devises indeed a great sin.
>
> (4:48)

If we worship or adore anything other than Allah, depend on anything other than Allah, wish anything other than the knowledge of Allah, then we have associated with Allah. The Prophet, describing association with Allah in a most profound and graphic way, said: "The creeping of association with Allah into my community is more hidden than the creeping of the black ant on a massive rock in the dark night." The meaning is that there are aspects of association, some gross, some much more subtle. Muslims tend to think that when they have eliminated the gross aspects there is nothing more to look for.

As for the injustice that will be forgiven, it is the injustice of the slave upon himself when he commits certain mistakes. If one transgresses upon oneself by forgetting the mercy of Allah, by having expectations and then being disappointed, one can immediately return, by the remembrance of Allah.

As for the injustice that cannot be left unpunished, it is when creational beings transgress against each other. The affliction and reprimand is harsh. If we abuse each other it will come

back upon us. No abuse will ever go unpunished. The punishment
may take time and it may take another form. It may be that we
are deprived of nature's restorative power. It may take the form
of other deprivations that we may not be able to measure or see.
The reaction to that unjust action may not be measurable quan-
titatively or qualitatively by our ways of measurement. Yet it
must exist, for nothing goes unheeded. We cannot escape anything in this life. Every action has an equal and opposite reaction.

The one who has denied recompense runs rampant and does
his utmost to create more excitement, more sensuality, more
acquisition, more arrogance and show of power. He has invested
in this outward, unrestrained expansion because he is ignorant
of the law of action-reaction and is ignorant of the Hereafter.
The man of Allah recognizes that he is constricted in this life.
He knows that he has come only to die, therefore what is the
point of accumulation? "This world is the prison for he who
trusts in Allah and the Hereafter and the Garden for the denier
with only a limited time."

Imam 'Ali, upon him be peace, tells us how to attain the
eternal Garden when he says: "Do not covet the things of this
world. Do not be greedy. Do not collect wealth, for you do not
know for whom you are collecting."

Look what happened almost immediately after the death of
the Prophet. When the nomadic bedouins suddenly saw wealth
pouring into the Muslim treasury, they realized the power of the
Prophet. Thousands upon thousands embraced Islam because
then they started to believe that this man was right. So, what
was it that drove them to it? It was the material world, which
was completely absent from the heart of Imam Husayn, that
brought them to Islam.

Another tradition from the Prophet's House states that, "He
is poor who has greed. He is wealthy who is content." This is
the contentment of the person who has done his best and his
utmost, having called upon his own heart and mind, and having
taken counsel.

We are constricted. We have certain bounds. Boundlessness
is an attribute of Allah. We are bondsmen or slaves, and that
bond is the way towards our freedom if we live it. This means

that we must not only recognize it intellectually but accept it totally, absolutely, unquestionably, as a bonded slave who is marked forever.

The way of the Prophet's House is based on the preference of the next life over this life. The Prophet says: "He who loves this world will affect his state in the Hereafter; and he who loves the Hereafter will affect his worldly existence. So prefer that which remains forever over that which will pass." We cannot have our cake and eat it. If one is a man of the Hereafter it shows in his actions. He moves like a straw in the wind of destiny, as Allah takes him, in contentment, and he who loves the Hereafter will reduce his worldy involvements. So there is a balance.

Regarding abandonment of the things of the world, Imam 'Ali said that the meaning of abandonment is not that one does not own anything, but rather that nothing owns him. If one has anything, using it in the way of Allah is a power, a useful power. The stronger believer is better than the weaker one, inwardly and outwardly.

The Prophet continues with the tradition: "Oh strange upon strangeness is it that he who believes or confirms the abode of foreverness rushes to enhance the home of arrogance." This typifies our case in the so-called Muslim world. Then he says: "He who goes about his life in this world, and is mainly concerned about his family, money, and home, has nothing with Allah. He will bring upon his heart four characteristics." We will digress here to recall that the Prophet said that all health is contingent upon the health of one's heart. If one's heart is not healthy, he will always be in affliction. Purification begins from the outward and works towards the inward.

Continuing with the four characteristics, the first is that: "He will be afflicted without any reprieve." For example, running from dawn to dusk trying to make ends meet with the excuse that we must get our children educated so that later they need to be de-brainwashed from the rubbish that has been poured into them, if they are so fortunate as to recognize the necessity of doing so. The second is: "Work that will never give them any time." There is no relief in the realm of chasing the world. One is always busy with his projects to the point that such involvement becomes an affliction. The third is: "Poverty that can never be enriched." What is enough in this type of system? One always finds oneself needing more. And the last is: "Constant hope for that house, that position, that acknowledgement, that respect, and on and on."

Then the Prophet said: "It is enough for you to have death as your preacher." If only one remembers death at every second, then one has access to life every second and goes beyond time to the One who encompasses time.

We have amongst the traditions of the Prophet's House the following: "There are people who worship Allah desiring mercy, and this is the worship of traders." In other words, their worship is a transaction, they exchange it for Mercy. "Other people worship Allah in fear of being chastised and that is the worship of slaves. And still others worship Allah in pure adoration and this is the worship of gratitude." Gratitude brings contentment of the heart and that is the state of the healthy heart. If the heart is content, then it is truly a heart, because it is turning. When the heart is discontented, it has ignorantly connected or attached itself to what has caused its discontent. Those who worship in gratitude, know that even their affliction is for their own good. Even if they do not recognize its meaning at that time, they have patience that they will come to know why it happened. They may have misjudged a situation, or invested in the wrong way, trusted other than Allah. Imam Husayn said: "Those who are in gratitude, this is worship for those who are free." They are free from other than Allah. This is the freedom which we are all seeking, the freedom of no choice.

Imam 'Ali, in a tradition regarding nature of what is decreed, quotes the Qur'an:

> No evil befalls the earth nor your own souls, but
> it is in a book (decreed) before We bring it into
> existence; surely that is easy to Allah.
> So that you may not grieve for what has escaped
> you, nor be exultant at what He has given you;
> and Allah does not love any arrogant boaster.
>
> (57:22-23)

Whatever afflicts us, in the earth or in ourselves, it is already in the Book, in the Eternal Book, the Book of Reality. It was there in the absolute, total decree before it was created. It was decreed in the sense that laws that govern this cosmos eventually will result in what you and I will experience — not decree in a superstitious sense. We are both free and chained. We are chained to the laws that govern existence and we are free to act within these constraints. The interaction of the two is what results in the dynamism of life. The Imam said this affliction was already there — it was already in the Book and we should not be sorry for what has happened. This world is a theatre, a facade. The test in this world is not to look back. Thus, the man of faith has all of his energies preserved. He is not sorry for what has happened for he has done his best.

The Prophet in response to being told about an occurrence, regardless of how distorted it was, would say not to look back upon it, do not feel sorry about it. Clean your heart and live in the present. That is the only contact point you have with Allah who is beyond time: now, now, now. The smaller that now is, the less it is in time.

Ignorance of how Allah's decree works is well explained in the following Qur'anic verse:

> And among men is he who says: We believe in Allah; but when he is persecuted in (the way of) Allah he thinks the persecution of men to be as the chastisement of Allah; and if there comes assistance from your Lord, they would most certainly say: Surely we were with you. What! Is not Allah the best Knower of what is in the breasts of mankind.
>
> (29:10)

Affliction is from the injustice of mankind. Man has the option as Allah's deputy on earth to handle or mishandle his representation so that he brings about justice or injustice. So, if we are afflicted by injustice it is our own doing. We have abused our authority, and we have not recognized that authority of Allah. We have not kept within the bounds of Allah, nor have we been in fearful awareness. The Prophet was asked on one occasion, "Who are the people of the (Prophet's) house?" He responded, "He who is in fearful awareness embraces that party."

The affliction of Karbala was the injustice of man upon man. All over the world people are constantly remembering events that help us to move more and more towards *tawhid* (unity), and one of the most remarkable of them all is the reactivation of Islam by the blood of the master Imam Husayn. Entry into his magnificent companionship can only be obtained by unifying the outer law of Islam with the inner reality. One must be a man of Allah inwardly and the most kind, gentle, understanding, compassionate, patient, and courageous man outwardly, willing to lay down one's life at any moment. When a person's will unifies with the will of God, then he enters into fighting in the way of Allah, the path of Imam Husayn. Then he is with the Imam at all times. His love of the Imam is transformed into the love of Allah, an uncompromising, absolute love born of total surrender.

17

The Meaning of Life and Death

Truly we ask Allah's forgiveness for not knowing His way, for not knowing the Imam of the day, for not following clearly and totally in the footsteps of the Prophet Muhammad. Allah is *al-Ghafur wa al-Rahim* (the All-Forgiving and Merciful) provided we truly stop our wrong actions. If we truly recognize how wrong we have been, then everything will be right. The reason we are suffering in this world is not because Allah wants us to suffer — Allah's creation is based on love. If we experience trouble and disagreement it is because we do not know the proper behaviour. I have come here to assert that the proper behaviour is the Muhammadi way. Having access to the Prophet Muhammad makes it easier for us to behave in a manner that will bring us success. And, along with what the Prophet has brought, we have the advantage of our knowledge of the Commander of the Faithful 'Ali, which in turn gives us access to all of the Imams after him.

This life is a preparation for the next: we have been brought here from the non-time to prepare ourselves spiritually for the Hereafter, which is also in the non-time.

This life is in the grip of Allah, but appears to be interfered with by man. Allah has given us limited freedom to see if we, like children at play, will make a mess of this world. But, in fact, he is in total control and he will not allow this world to fall into the hands of the violent. This world will end up in the hands of the people of light and the Muslims. Not the Muslims whom we commonly refer to, but the Muslims who have actually submitted, awakened and are living every second. If one lives every second to its fullness, one is already on the edge of non-time, tasting the meaning of infinity, smelling the Garden. One of the names of the Garden is *Khuld* (endless time) derived from the word *khalid* (everlasting, permanent). Its verbal root is *khalada* and yields two meanings. The first one is 'to take refuge', 'to settle in', such as settling in a house. The second meaning is 'to last forever', Allah is *al-Khalid*, 'The Everlasting'.

All of us are lovers of Allah, whether we know it or not. We love His attributes. We love His names, *al-Khalid* (the Everlasting), *al-Baqi* (the Permanent), *al-Samad* (He on Whom All Depend). Because we do not want to be dependent on anybody, we pervertedly bite the hand that feeds us. We yearn to feel secure and independent. But we are all dependent on food, water, air, and ultimately upon Allah at every moment.

We find confirmation of our dependence upon the perfect Creator when we examine the human body. Our blood goes through vessels whose total length adds up to about 1600 to 1800 miles. There are millions of chemical reactions taking place within us. How do they work? How do our eyes, and our nervous system function? How is it possible for us to coordinate our hands. Is not our body incredible? Yet we take it for granted. We are in *ghaflah*, which means distraction, and it occurs when something makes look in the wrong direction. Because we are not aware, Shaytan (Satan) is allowed to enter our life transaction. One of the words for awareness in Arabic is *dhikr* which also means remembrance. So unawareness is a failure to remember. But what are we to remember? The Qur'an gives us the answer — it tells us we have to remember and why we have to remember. Allah says in Qur'an:

> Now surely by Allah's remembrance are the hearts
> set at rest.
>
> (13:28)

Certainly it is by remembrance, by recalling, by calling upon Allah that the hearts will find calm.

Now what is the remembrance of Allah? Our Prophet says in a *hadith* (one of his sayings) that we are not to talk about Allah, rather we are to discuss His attributes. How can we discuss His essence? But we can talk about His attributes, His actions, and His creation.

> Surely We have shown him the way: he may be
> thankful or unthankful.
>
> (76:3)

If man is grateful towards what Allah has shown him, he increases. If he rejects the truth, he is diminished and is doomed. Even if it is a whole nation that is ungrateful and thereby rejects the truth, Allah says He will recycle them:

> Surely this is easy for Allah.
>
> (35:11)

And the Qur'an says that Allah will bring together a people who love Him and whom He loves. Allah promises that His light will spread throughout His creation.

What is this light that is spoken of by Allah? It is not the sun nor any physical manifestation. The light of Allah is the knowldge of Allah, contained within His laws. These laws manifest on many levels, the grossest being on the physical. Within the physical world the laws of gravity are not going to change. Thank God for that. Allah says in the Qur'an:

> Such has been the course of Allah that has indeed run before, and you shall not find a change in Allah's course.
>
> (48:23)

Allah is not going to change His course, his *sunnah*, simply because we have been nice people. We will be recycled like all of the rest of mankind if we are among the messy. So it is up to us to purify ourselves and place ourselves within the company of the right people with the right intention. Allah is not going to reprieve you simply because you have prayed five times a day and then performed your fast.

If you have true Faith, then you trust Allah. And even if you are collapsing, you are still content, saying ' "*al-hamdu lillah* (Glory be to Allah), I am in Allah's hand and He is my master.' You are not afraid of anything. If you have *iman* (belief, faith, trust) and *'aql* (the faculty of reasoning) you are able to distinguish between people. You know when the people you are with are cheating each other. You perceive that there is no harmony, no unity. There is no good leader for them to follow. They are in a mess and if you are with them, you are in a mess. This is the situation unless one of us emerges to live as though at any time

Imam 'Ali will walk in and will ask us: 'Why are you not sincere to each other? Why are you not honest with each other?'

Imam 'Ali himself said, when asked why he did not claim his right to the caliphate: "Give me forty men." The meaning of his answer is that at the time there were not forty men who would follow him. We have to realize the situation as it is, otherwise, we will constantly be disappointed. But this does not mean that we should give up in despair. No, Allah says in the Qur'an:

> I will not take from you a sign unless I replace it
> with a better one.
>
> (8:70)

This means, among other things, that our time now is better. It is not better in the outward sense, for outwardly it is worse. We find every year is outwardly more difficult, more complicated, more cumbersome than the year before. But if one is a believer and one's intellect is growing with one's faith, every year one acquires more wisdom, more understanding, more compassion. So, although outwardly we may be worse off with each passing year — we are getting older and our teeth are falling out — inwardly we are improving as we draw closer to the end of this short journey, if we have prepared ourselves by truly following Imam 'Ali, who said: "O world! I have divorced you." He meant: 'I am not going to fall into distraction. The world is not going to dazzle me.' The Imam uses the example of a woman because a woman's job is to attract man in order to maintain the continuity of this creation. Her nature is to attract man in order for her to procreate and to stabilize the family because man is, in a sense, unstable. So when he says that he has divorced the world, he does not mean that he has kicked it aside, for he relies on this world for sustenance. He means that he is on earth not being choked by the *dunya*, by the material world and its concerns. Among the related meanings spinning off from *dana*, which is the root word of *dunya*, are 'near and close'. So we see that *dunya*, this world, is close and therefore easily tricks us. This world is attractive to us because it catches our attention before anything else.

Distinguishing between the *dunya* (the material world) and the *ardh* (the earth) we see that the *ardh* belongs to Allah, is His garden and is neutral, whereas the *dunya* is what we make of this world. If we are attached to it then it is *dunya*. Imam 'Ali defines *zuhd* as being free of material oppression. The *zahid*, the one who practises *zuhd*, is pious, implying a certain measure of independence from the world and its attraction. When he says: "Doing without does not mean that you do not own anything, but means that nothing owns you.' A very subtle distinction is made. One may have material means, but to be defined as free of them one must put them to their proper use. We may enjoy the things of this world as we make our way toward the Hereafter, aware that this world is full of tricks and pitfalls. So we do not renounce the world, rather we renounce the *dunya:* we renounce our attachment to the world. There is nothing wrong with a fine house or a beautiful garden or a comfortable place. What is wrong is our becoming a slave to them, and not being able to move away from them. There is nothing wrong with a decent meal. What is wrong is my constant expectation of a two-course or three-course or four-course meal. This is where the trouble lies. And if we are not aware of what goes on in ourselves, no matter how many outwardly correct acts of the *shari'ah* we perform, we will not be in *tawhid* because our interior will not be unified with our exterior. The lack of unification in our lives is causing us to suffer and the lack of unification in the so-called Muslim enclaves or countries is causing a whole people to suffer.

To reach *tawhid* we have a formula which is: begin by proclaiming *tawhid* outwardly. As the Qur'an says:

> And your garments do purify.
>
> (74:4)

We begin by purifying our clothes until such time as our hearts are pure, are unattached. And then through a constant revolution, through a constant turning of the heart we reach *tawhid*. The word for heart itself is *qalb*, and its verbal root is *qalaba* which means 'to revolve, to turn'. The implication is that a true heart is not attached. Knowing this we next can see how this

principle was exemplified by the Prophet. Whenever he was
approached and told that a certain event had happened, he
would accept it unconditionally. He would never look back, nor
blame people for what they had done. He would be absolutely
efficient, retaining all of his energies to move into the correct
future. Such was the state of that perfect being. His heart at all
times was available and a reflector of the truth. It reflected
reality, Allah's reality. And likewise, this is the state of the man
who has abandoned himself to Allah, which is the meaning of
the word 'Muslim'. We say we are Muslims in the hope that it
becomes real, outwardly and inwardly, without any differentiation between outer and inner.

I wanted to share with you an open secret which is Allah's
secret. Where is it that He is not? Where is it that the heart of
the believer does not find confirmation of Allah's permanent
perfection?

I want to share with you an advantage that the followers of
the Imams have. It is our fearlessness in the face of death. It is
a current message now in newspapers and elsewhere that the
lovers of the Imams are suicidal, that the Shi'ah people in south
Lebanon are suicidal and of course terrorists. The media have
labelled a hundred and fifty million people as terrorists. Now I
want to share with you the meaning of their willingness to die
from a spiritual point of view. I want to show you from the
Qur'an that if we truly believe in the next life, we will be in
constant remembrance of death and that this remembrance will
not make us heavy-hearted, on the contrary, if we are true believers it will make us alive. Every second will be an infinity. Every
breath will be beyond time. Then we will be in this life without
belonging to it, knowing the meaning of the *barzakh*, the interspace of intermediary world. With the remembrance or death
we look to where we are going. It is something that we have
actually tasted already in the form of sleep. Sleep is a mini-death
and we have a peculiar love and attraction to it. We are programmed to love death, if only we knew what it meant. I have collected
for you a few hadiths (sayings of the Prophet) and a few *ayats*
of the Qur'an to show you how important it is for the believer
to remember death.

Islam has the science of abandonment and freedom, not the science of mucking about with the lower self. I was once giving a talk in Karachi about the magnificent heritage of remembering death which makes you instantly less selfish and more humble. During the talk a psychologist who was disturbed by what I was saying said, "Isn't it morbid talking about death? We want to cheer people up and make them happy." In Islam there is no psychology in the western sense because the self which it deals with, the headstrong self or the self that directs us to do evil *(an-nafs al-ammara bisu')*, is not an acceptable subject to focus upon.

There is inward happiness as well as outward happiness. At best, the people of *dunya*, those attached to the life of this world, will obtain a taste of other happiness. But we want eternal joy which is the result of abandoning ourselves to Allah on the path of Islam, by means of submission, faith, trust, belief and excellence. Why hide the fact that we are all dying? Every breath is taking us closer to it. The only correct statement every human being can make at any time is: I am closer to death. While at one moment you may be happy, the next moment you may be unhappy, and so on. Yet, the psychologist wants the Muslim to forget it. Forgetting death only serves to enrich the drug companies who issue drugs to stop people from being connected.

I want to share with you this incredible formula that the people of Allah have, which is the remembrance of death. In this way we will not only be prepared for death but prepared for what is beyond it. Our formula is to live in the knowledge that at any moment we may be called to account for our actions. I want to read first from the Qur'an on the subject of death.

> Say: If the future abode with Allah is specially for
> you to the exclusion of (other) people, then invoke
> death if you are truthful.
>
> (2:94)

Allah says: If you truly talk about the next life and you are sincere about it, and you think it belongs to you, and you claim it is specially reserved for you to the exclusion of others, then if you are truthful, you would wish for death. Also Allah says:

> And they will never invoke it on account of what
> their hands have sent before, and Allah knows the
> unjust.
>
> (2:95)

Those people who claim the next world over others will in fact
never wish for death because of what their hands have done.
The meaning of "what their hands have sent" is what our life
is: what we are doing and what is important to us, what we give
and take and what we discard. Also in *Surah al-Jumu'ah* we read
the following:

> Say: O you who are Jews, if you think that you
> are the favourites of Allah to the exclusion of other
> people, then invoke death if you are truthful. And
> they will never invoke it because of what their
> hands have sent before; and Allah is Cognizant of
> the unjust.
>
> (62:6–7)

The *ayah* specifically addresses the Jews. In Arabic the phrase
al-ladhina hadu (those who are guided, the Jews) is connected
with *huda* 'to be guided'. Ironically, Allah says in the next *ayah*
that they can never wish for death because they (the Jews) are
lovers of the *dunya*. The Prophet says: "The *dunya* is for the
unbelievers a garden and for the believers a prison." The unbeliever only knows about beautiful little houses, so that is all he
gets. The believer has recognized and has been exposed to the
light of Allah and because of that he feels imprisoned in this
world. At all times the believer is outwardly in *jihad*, struggling
in the way of Allah; at all times he tries his best to share the
incredible gift of the knowledge that we are returning to Him
after we leave this world. He knows that we are watched even
though we cannot see the Watcher. This is called *maqam al-ihsan*,
the station of goodness.

So in the above *ayah* Allah is saying that those who call themselves Jews do not believe and will not relinquish their hold on
this world. Now the point is that this *ayah* is not limited to any
historical context. As it applies to the Jews, so it applies to us

even though we may have been born in Islam. Allah says in the Qur'an:

> But none feels secure from the plot of Allah except
> the people who shall perish.
>
> (7:99)

Never say: 'I am a believer' and feel content and safe. Where is the end of *iman* (faith)? *"Al-imanu darajat"* (faith is in degrees). What we may say is: 'Allah forgive us our faults, remind us of them and cause us to move in a positive direction.' In addition, we may be proud of our heritage of Islam and of our love of the Imams (the descendants of the Prophets) whom we intend to follow as though they were with us, as though any one of them may visit us at any time.

Allah is challenging those who pretend, those who are hypocritical. He says: "If you truly mean what you say, then wish for death." Therefore the true believer views his short life as an experiment and as a test. At any moment he is ready to leave, ready to return his body back to where it belongs, which is to the soil and the worms and the scorpions.

> And they ask you about the soul. Say: The soul is
> one of the commands of my Lord, and you are not
> given aught of knowledge but a little.
>
> (17:85)

They ask you the meaning of *ruh*. It is by command of Allah. *"Kun fayakun"* (Be and it is). So look! the *ruh* is free. If we do not unify these aspects, we will not taste the sweetness of faith. Until then we will not take to the practises of Islam. It is no use forcing our children to practise Islam if we ourselves have not transmitted its sweetness to them.

We hold on to that which is superficial, outward, and institutional without freeing the heart from the drudgery of its attachment to the *dunya*. It is no use denouncing the corruption of the people in Muslim countries. If they look at their own situation, they will see that their only joy is in grabbing money. If they could find joy in witnessing the incredible nature of the creation, and the fact that it, in a sense, hides the Creator, they would not go for the lesser joys which are available to them. Once the heart is open to the highest of joys, man cannot be bought, even if he were to be offered all the kingdoms in creation. The believer realizes the truth of Imam 'Ali's words: "He who performs good deeds is accountable for them and his evil actions will bring punishment upon him." All our actions are taken into account by the One who is the most efficient banker, Allah. Is our inward knowledge and outward action unified? If not, we cannot talk about Islam which is submission, giving in to the *wahid al-ahad* (the One and Only). There are over two and a half million Muslims from the Indian sub-continent living in England, yet very few of the native English have become Muslims. If the Muslims were truly unified with the meaning of what they call themselves, England would now be dominated by Islam. If the English were given the key to the inner garden, if they came to know the meaning of submission and faith and the joy of it, would they continue to poison themselves by frequenting the pubs? The fact that very few English men and women have become Muslims means that the so-called Muslims who live among them are Muslim in name only. Islam is about the knowledge of Allah. If Islam is not leading you to the gate of that knowledge, then you are following something else.

The test in this life is to be willing, joyfully, to face death because the believer has not only the knowlege but the truth of certainty — *al-haqq al-yaqin* — and that is his freedom. He sees himself as one placed in a cage training for his flight to freedom through death. Just as the young bird is prepared slowly for its eventual flight into the air, so he is prepared for death through his acquisiton of discrimination, by the development of his capacity to reason, and by bearing witness that there is nothing in this life that is going to give him true joy. In this life we busy ourselves with a job, a house, a spouse. No matter how we try to manage and balance our entire situation, we fail but for brief moments — until we learn the key to our real satisfaction. Through knowledge we learn to be content in every situation because we see how events occur. We see the laws of Allah. We may be outwardly afflicted, but inwardly we see perfect creational harmony and ecology. When we have attained this, then we are prepared for that incredible flight which takes place at the point of death.

In Arabic, in addition to the word *mawt* (death), the word *wafah* (death) is used. *Wafa'* has another meaning, 'loyalty', and occurs in the Qur'an in many instances with this meaning. For example, in *Surah al-Zumar* Allah says:

> Allah takes the souls at the time of their death.
>
> (39:42)

Literally this may be paraphrased, 'Allah will cause the *nafs* to be in *wafa'* when it dies.' We are loyal to our Creator, whether we know it or not, because we are going to return to Him. Both the spirit and the body are loyal. The body is loyal to the earth because since it has escaped from it, its return is inevitable. The spirit's *wafa'* (loyalty) depends on its spiritual elevation: it is determined by whether or not it has risen to what it has been created for.

Allah says:

> And Allah has created you, then He causes you to die, and many a one of you is reduced in old age to most abject state, so that after having knowledge he does not know anything; surely Allah is Knowing, Powerful.
>
> (16:70)

All this is to test your loyalty, sincerity, honesty and faith.

> Do they not consider how many a generation We have destroyed before them, whom We had established in the earth as We have not established you, and We sent the clouds pouring rain on them in abundance, and We made the rivers to flow beneath them, then we destroyed them on account of their faults and raised up after them another generation.
>
> (6:6)

Allah also says that he gives us, in this life, the experience of death. Sleep is that experience, it is a mini-death. Our longing for death is attested to by our love for sleep. The more tired we become, the more we yearn to taste our mini-death.

The mercy of the Compassionate One prepares us to take off in the next life, the *akhirah*. When we come to death, it will not be the "affliction...combined with affliction" (75:29) experienced by those who do not wish to die. On the contrary, when we meet death our experience will be like that of the real believers. How beautifully they die! Look at the death of the Master of All Believers, Imam 'Ali ibn Abi Talib. He said: "I have won, by the Lord of the Ka'bah!" But who was he referring to when he said 'I'? Was it the social security number or 'Ali the ex-husband of Fatimah? No, it was the voice of the *ruh*, the soul, with the cry of triumph. The soul was expressing its triumph at its loss of its body. Both the soul and the body were returning to their sources. It was easy and spontaneous. It is only when a man wishes to hold onto his body, not permitting his soul and body to separate, that death is hard. To facilitate this separation we use, before our death, a simple formula which is the remembrance of death.

Our master, the Prophet Muhammad, said, "Death is enough of a warning." The warner says, "Don't be angry. Don't be in haste." If you remember death while you are angry, you will be ashamed of yourself. Imagine cheating someone or being suspicious of someone and death comes to you. It is for this reason that we visit the great masters' graves. We do not worship them. The grave is nothing other than a hole. But when we go to the grave of a great being such as an Imam, we remember what he represents, how he lived, and how he died. We remember that he was an *ayah*, a sign of Allah on this earth, and we want to aspire towards that and follow in his footsteps. If we don't go there, we go somewhere else less important, which is less of a reminder. That is the reason the Prophet says: "Increase the remembrance of death for its remembrance obliterates one's mistakes and makes one renounce pleasure in worldly things." It helps to obliterate our mistakes as we have just discovered. Also he says it does not make you insecure about this world. You take what you can, you do your best. And you have no fear. Incidentally, if you have less fear and anxiety about the *dunya* it will be easier to accept it, because your efficiency will increase. Also the Prophet says: "Death is the believer's treasure." He says that because this world is the believers prison, within which there is nothing but affliction and turmoil. Peace, in the true sense, is never obtained here. *Salam* is one of the names of Allah. We love peace, and thus, whether we like it or not, we love Allah. Even the *kuffar* (the rejectors of truth) love Allah. The vacations which they take are rituals undertaken out of love for *Salam*. Because they do not know that the key to *salam* is the heart, they travel and often, on their return, they more fully appreciate their home because of the miserable time that they had while on vacation.

Every man is a lover of Allah whether he knows it or not. The believer knows it and so is unified. The *kafir* (disbeliever) or the *munafiq* (hypocrite) or the *mushrik* (those who worship others with Allah) does not know it, therefore he is confused. If we truly have faith in Islam and act righteously, we are never confused.

And then also the Prophet said: "Remember more of that which destroyed pleasures, remember death." By remembering death we will not always be running after wordly pleasures. He also said: "If the cattle had the capacity to know what the son of Adam (man) knows about death, you would never have eaten one of them which was fat." All of them would be agile, ready and aware of the next life.

A man from the *Ansar* (those who supported the Prophet in Medina) came to the Prophet and asked him: "Who is the most generous and wisest of all men?" The Prophet answered: "Those people who remember death most, and those who are most ready for it." We are not suicidal, nor are we here to disturb anything. We are here to know the key which will give us inner peace. We are here to serve Allah in His creation and to be the slaves and the servant of his most perfect creation, the Prophet. Allah told the Messenger:

> And We have not sent you but as a mercy to the worlds.
>
> (21:107)

We are not here to cause a disturbance, nor are we here to occupy ourselves with the life of this world. Our job is to be ready so that we are not scared when the day comes. Every one of us will be driving into death with a smile on our face. This, the unbeliever and the worshipper of many gods cannot understand. They are veiled from reality. Our master, Imam 'Ali, who is the door to the city of knowledge, said: "I advise you to remember death and reduce your forgetfulness of it." The key is the reality of *la ilaha*. Stop hanging on to what is temporal. Stop forgetting death. And he says: "How can you be forgetful about something that itself does not forget you?" He continued by saying: "How can you be courteous about something that will never give you respite?" The Prophet was asked: "Who is the most *zahid* of people?" In other words, who is the person who is the least attached to this world? He said: "He who does not forget the grave."

Lastly, I shall mention what the Prophet said concerning how one is to remember the next life. He said: "He who leaves the outer frivolity, the unimportant things of this *dunya* (who takes what he needs, for his strength, for his knowledge, for his heart), who prefers that which remains to that which will be destroyed and never counts tomorrow as one of his days (because it has not come) but counts himself as one of the people of the graves (i.e. dead)." 'Ali Zayn al-'Abidin, in one of his supplications, says: "Oh Allah make me not think that the next breath will follow this one and do not make me think that one leg will follow the other as I move it." This is *dhikr* (remembrance), which brings total awareness and beingness. This is our heritage, not arguments about this or that. If we do not move to that core, we will remain chasing our tails around in a circle, getting nowhere. The Prophet said that we should not count tomorrow as one of our days but rather we should consider ourselves as among the people of the graves.

Another hadith from the Prophet containing the same meaning is: "If you want to look at a dead person walking, look at me." But he was the most vital of all living beings. So what does this hadith mean? It means that his heart was dead to attachment, expectation, rancour, jealousy, and backbiting. It was a reflector of the Pure Reality that brought about all the other reflectors, among of whom we are representatives. Each reflector is only as good as the degree of its polishing. When we are tarnished by fears, anxieties, expectations and jealousies, we are unable to fully reflect the Reality. So we are lovers of the remembrance of death because we are lovers of the Creator of death who has also created life. For this reason we cry when a child is born, we foresee the trouble that it is going to have. We are happy when somebody dies; we say that now he knows the truth. This is our heritage, the knowledge and experience of which we are proud. The traditions are of no use if they are mentioned but not performed. It is like cooking a meal: if we do not know how to cook our own meal, we will do nothing but read and talk about the recipes and menus. But there is no use being angry about it. Let us do something. Let every one of us rise above being critical. There is no point in us saying all the time that it is their fault. What good is it doing us? We are being destroyed, not remade. We are not making ourselves ready for the next life. By blaming others, we are missing an incredibel opening in this life and in the next.

What I have been describing is the true way. We want to be able to embrace it and know that it is our survival kit so that we can move on, unafraid of death, but afraid of transgressing Allah's laws. We are only afraid of ignorance. This is the true state of the Muslim.

I hope we have managed to share with each other a tiny drop of the incredible ocean of the way to live, the way to be — the way to be in this life and yet not belong to it, because we belong to the *akhirah* (the next life). We are the people who move ahead in this life, joyfully, openly, cheerfully, objectively, honestly, waiting for the openings from Allah, who will give us the knowledge that will prepare us for what is to come. I pray that Allah will take our hands and guide us higher and higher by Him to Him. I pray that everyone of us will be attracted to the true knowledge of our heritage and will embrace it.

May Allah bless you and transform your intentions into correct actions. May Allah give us the light of Islam. May Allah increase the love of the Prophet Muhammad in our hearts. May Allah give us the opportunity of serving completely in the way of Allah. May our gatherings at all times be in the remembrance of Allah. May Allah make those gatherings so useful that we may even see the results in our own lifetime.